Twelve Qualities

of the

Successful Plaintiff

Tamara Kismet

DEDICATION

This book is dedicated to my mother and father, without whose sacrifices, I would never have been able to go to law school.

CONTENTS

Learning about the legal system is somewhat like climbing a mountain. At the base of the mountain, the view isn't so spectacular. All you see before you is a wall of granite. And just as that imposing wall can appear difficult to climb, our legal system can seem difficult to understand.

But with stamina and determination, you can conquer those sheer walls of rock, one ledge at a time. Similarly, you can learn to navigate our legal system as a successful plaintiff, one step at a time. As your guide, I'll take you up this "mountain" by a gentle and easy path. I know all the shortcuts and hazards on this mountain because I've climbed it many times myself. But since this mountain is unfamiliar territory for many readers, I'll keep things on a level that's easy to follow.

I think you're going to find this climb to be a satisfying, exhilarating, and educational experience. And when we get to the top of the mountain, I genuinely believe you'll enjoy a panoramic "view" that will provide valuable insight into handling your legal affairs.

Tamara Kismet

Introduction

"There is no such thing as justice - in or out of court."

Clarence Darrow

It's funny that you've picked up a book about how to be a successful plaintiff. After all, there are tons of books out there about how to be a healthier person, smarter parent, or better lover. Why would anyone even CARE about what it takes to be a successful plaintiff? To some, the very notion can seem offensive.

But there's nothing offensive about learning how to be a *successful plaintiff*. It's simply a matter of protecting your rights in a legal system which has become aggressive and hostile towards the average person. Our society has moved in a direction that forces people to fight for their rights with increasing regularity. When that happens, people are introduced to a legal system that isn't necessarily "user-friendly." It's a system that can be a tricky maze for the uninitiated. It's filled with traps and pitfalls for the unwary. It's fraught with inconsistencies, double standards, and hypocrisy.

The famous trial attorney Clarence Darrow probably summed it up best when he said, "There is no such thing as justice - in or out of court." This is the observation of a man who was recognized as one of the most brilliant trial attorneys of his day. And there's no shortage of evidence to prove him correct. Look at our criminal justice system. Stealing a loaf of bread from a supermarket will bring heavy-handed punishment to a common thief, while robbing the American people of millions as a corporate executive can provide a very comfortable lifestyle.

Look at our civil justice system. We see plaintiffs with questionable injuries treated like martyrs, enjoying insane settlement awards that could be described more as lottery jackpots than reasonable compensation for the harm they actually suffered. And on the flip side, we see plaintiffs who suffer unspeakable harm walk away from court with nothing. What does it show, other than the fact that maybe there really is no such thing as justice.

It shows that people who know how to use the legal system to their advantage succeed. And it isn't necessarily about wealth or power. Yes, there are situations where wealth can pave the way for success in a courtroom. But in the big picture, success as a plaintiff mainly depends upon possessing the right qualities. Certain *qualities* can enable someone to prevail in this game which is as much psychological as it is intellectual.

Plaintiffs who possess these qualities often succeed, while plaintiffs who do not are frustrated by this same system. Our legal system is far from

2

perfect. It may not be fair. It may not be logical. It may not be consistent. Yet it's still a system that affords plaintiffs some element of control over the course of events, provided they know HOW to conduct themselves.

This book focuses on twelve qualities of successful plaintiffs. These qualities are listed below:

(1.) The successful plaintiff picks battles carefully.

(2.) The successful plaintiff exploits an adversary's weaknesses.

(3.) The successful plaintiff possesses a plaintiff's attitude.

(4.) The successful plaintiff chooses a good attorney, if necessary.

(5.) The successful plaintiff possesses persistence and determination.

(6.) The successful plaintiff is not held back by fear.

(7.) The successful plaintiff understands the power of perception.

(8.) The successful plaintiff practices the golden rule.

(9.) The successful plaintiff understands the art of negotiation.

(10.) The successful plaintiff adapts to factors that cannot be controlled.

(11.) The successful plaintiff conducts business with politeness and professionalism.

(12.) The successful plaintiff enjoys some element of luck.

Okay, so you say these twelve qualities are all very nice to read about. But why should they mean anything to someone who has no intention of ever becoming a plaintiff? Well, just take a look around. With minor exceptions, most plaintiffs you see out there never really set out *intending* to be plaintiffs. They became plaintiffs because they were injured.

They became plaintiffs because they were wronged by government programs that were supposed to help them. They became plaintiffs because an employer couldn't resist being mean-spirited toward them. They became plaintiffs because they were cheated by someone in a business transaction. When you look at the direction our society is taking, you realize that chances for becoming a plaintiff of some kind are fairly good.

What are the benefits of knowing how to be a *successful plaintiff?* The benefits can mean prevailing in a lawsuit. Are people who obtain the largest settlement awards in personal injury cases truly the ones who sustained the most severe injuries? Perhaps, but not always. Are people who retire on disability benefits more deserving than their disabled co-workers who stick it out for 15 more years on the job? Perhaps, but not always. Are people who succeed in wrongful termination actions truly the ones who were most maliciously wronged by their employers? Perhaps, but not always. But it IS safe to say that all such people possessed qualities that made them well-suited to navigate our legal system as *successful plaintiffs*.

By culture, most people are not naturally inclined to be *successful plaintiffs*. It's simply not engrained in us. We plan how to be *successful grandparents* by preparing well-drafted wills and estate plans for our families. We plan how to be *successful entrepreneurs* by choosing to run a business as a limited liability corporation rather than a sole proprietorship. We plan how to be *successful inventors* by protecting our clever ideas with patents. But we rarely plan for what to do if we found ourselves in the position of *plaintiff.*

You might say there isn't much to think about here. If you find yourself in the position of plaintiff, you simply put yourself in the hands of a good attorney. The right attorney is the ingredient that makes one a *successful plaintiff.* While that may be true, it's only partly true. Just as people can be better patients for their doctors, they can be better clients for their attorneys.

An attorney is a counselor, not a parent. A good attorney advises a client about various options in a given situation, outlining the advantages and disadvantages of each. But it's always the client's call to choose the best course of action. Possessing the qualities described in this book can enable a plaintiff to make such choices with better insight.

Another thing about attorneys is that not every plaintiff runs to one at the first sign of trouble. While that's a personal decision for which there are pros and cons, some people like to explore options that don't include an attorney. Some like to see how far they can take a legal matter before calling in the cavalry. Some like to save money by handling their own legal fights. Some have concerns that attorneys can turn small problems into big problems, just to generate legal fees. Some people simply despise attorneys and are willing do everything in their power not to hire one unless there's absolutely no other choice.

As far as hiring professional help goes, people are more sophisticated nowadays when it comes to legal matters. There's no shortage of legal self-help material on the internet, at bookstores, or local libraries. There are templates for legal forms. There are video tutorials. These have served to demystify many areas of law for the public at large. And they have enabled people to be more self-reliant in their legal affairs.

For all these reasons, people could have strong incentives to understand what it takes to be a *successful plaintiff*. Possessing the qualities of a successful plaintiff could mean the difference between settling a legal matter for $2,500, or taking it to a jury trial for a $65,000 verdict. It could also mean making a good decision to walk away from bringing a lawsuit in the first place. Or it could mean finding a less painful alternative to a long and bitter battle in divorce court.

Knowing how to be a *successful plaintiff* can be good for one's personal life, business affairs, and emotional well-being. And that's what this book is about. It's a short book. But it covers lots of information. I think you'll revisit it to reread certain chapters more than once. I think you're going to learn a lot… and you're going to have fun doing so! Good luck, and enjoy!

How Does Someone Become a Plaintiff?

"A lost battle is a battle one thinks one has lost."

Jean-Paul Sartre

How does someone become a plaintiff? That isn't a lawyer joke waiting for a punch line. It's a question that's close to home for many people. Let's look at the different ways. A carpenter falls off a scaffold at work and finds his role in life transformed from proud family breadwinner to that of homebound invalid.

The "company store" doctor says he can return to work after 30 days, despite his severe injuries. People in the carpenter's position are often pushed back to work by such "company store" doctors, whether they're able to work or not. The carpenter now faces a dilemma. He'll have no paycheck if he stays home, or he'll compound his injuries if he returns to work. The hopeless situation forces him to explore legal options. A plaintiff has been created.

How does someone become a plaintiff? A supervisor puts in thirty years with a large corporation. She becomes a target of harassment after complaining about staying late to do inventory "off the clock." But such practices are not uncommon today, as employers tend to expect more from their people in a bad economy. The practice is stressful on employees. On one hand, people want to keep their jobs. On the other, no one likes to work for free. It has to be confusing for the corporations as well. One minute, they're dealing with young girls in third world countries who work long hours without complaining. The next, they're dealing with forty-something single moms in developed countries who want to be paid for the hours they work. Our supervisor is left with no other choice but to explore her legal options against the unpaid overtime policy. A plaintiff has been created.

How does someone become a plaintiff? A teacher loses her job because a student falsely claimed she made sexual advances toward him. You know the rules in our society. If a child accuses an adult, treat the adult as guilty unless she can prove herself innocent. The school district pushes the teacher out of her job because of pressure from militant parents in the community. Attorneys for the school district feel comfortable that the teacher will bow her head in shame and leave quietly. Instead, she comes back with all guns blazing. She files a wrongful termination lawsuit against the school district and a defamation lawsuit against the student for the malicious and cruel accusations. A plaintiff has been created.

How does someone become a plaintiff? The wife of a hardworking auto mechanic winds up in the hospital for six months after a bout with cancer. With his $16 an hour salary, the mechanic has trouble staying ahead of mortgage payments, hospital bills, and credit card bills. He has health insurance, but the hospital steadily sends him a mountain of bills for services that are denied by his insurance carrier. He puts the bills on his credit cards and obligingly pays them. But after a year of this financial strain, he has three credit cards stretched to the limit. He is behind on mortgage payments. He faces collection actions from two law firms. When he consults with credit counselors, he is told that filing for bankruptcy is his best course of action. A plaintiff has been created.

How does someone become a plaintiff? Two former college classmates partner up and launch their own advertising agency. But after working together for three years, they find themselves fighting in court. They both worked hard to build the business. They developed advertising campaigns together. They cultivated clients together. However, one of them decided he would be wealthier without a partner. Rather than doing the decent thing and telling his partner he wants out, he does something else. He funnels work away from the agency to a new company formed by his girlfriend. It isn't a nice thing to do, but this kind of thing happens when someone feels that two loaves are better than one. The wronged partner sees the situation as a hopeless mess, where his partner's deceit would be too difficult to prove. However, after assessing things with a calm head, he realizes there is adequate evidence to construct a case against his former partner. A plaintiff has been created.

How does someone become a plaintiff? A hardworking cashier is struck by a car as she crosses the street on her way home from work. She is seriously injured and cannot return to work. To make matters worse, she receives a $2,400 bill from the hospital emergency room. She approaches the driver's insurance company and asks them to pay her medical bills and lost wages. Instead of helping her, the insurance company launches an investigation. They question her immigration status. They ask her to provide pay stubs, which she is unable to do because the employer pays her cash. The insurance company blames the accident on her own inattention while crossing the street. She is left in the position of having no income, owing the hospital money, and having no means of paying for additional medical care she seriously needs. Having no other choice, she goes after the driver in court. At that point, the driver's insurance company reluctantly steps up to the plate. A plaintiff has been created.

And these are just a few ways in which people can become plaintiffs. They're close to home for many people. But society has trained us to think of plaintiffs as something different... more along the lines of people who pretend to slip on banana peels in shopping malls to pursue bogus lawsuits. That's an inaccurate depiction. Those clowns are still out there, but they make up a very small sector of plaintiffs at large. People can become plaintiffs for a million different reasons, often reluctantly.

Whether the problem is a difficult employer, deceitful business partner, bad accident, misconduct by a powerful organization, or financial problems, we see that bad things can happen to good people. Becoming a plaintiff isn't something people generally choose to do. But it is something they're sometimes *forced* to do when life throws a vicious curve ball their way.

And that's why it's important to know about what it takes to be a *successful plaintiff*. And that's why I wrote this book... to teach you those things!

The Successful Plaintiff Picks Battles Carefully

"This is a court of law, young man, not a court of justice."

Oliver Wendell Holmes, Supreme Court Justice

The successful plaintiff does something very important before the first step is even taken in a legal matter. That *something* has nothing to do with mapping out a brilliant courtroom strategy. It has nothing to do with finding the most aggressive attorney within a 100 mile radius. That *something* is almost proverbial in nature.

A successful plaintiff follows the rule that it's important to pick your battles. There's no point fighting a legal battle you can't win. And there's no point winning a legal battle that costs more than it's worth. When reviewing a legal matter, a successful plaintiff performs a simple test, made up of two elements. The first element is whether the matter has *merit*. This means there is something valid that justifies legal action. No one wants to be the state's most passionate plaintiff in a lawsuit that will be dismissed by a judge. The second element is, "How much is at stake?" In legal terms, this element is known as *damages*.

Let's illustrate the concept. John Doe is involved in a car accident. After getting out of the emergency room, he schedules an appointment with an attorney at a local law firm. The attorney considers two elements in deciding whether to accept or decline the case. First she reviews the police report. It shows that John Doe was sitting at a red light when another car hit him from the rear. This means the other driver was liable. *Liable* is a 75¢ legal term for *being at fault*. Since John Doe is not at fault, his case has strong *merit*. Next, the attorney examines the *damages* in John Doe's case. She reviews hospital records and medical reports. If John Doe hasn't sustained significant *damages* (in the form of injuries) she'll decline the case, despite its strong *merit*.

This basic analysis is used by attorneys across the world. But it doesn't apply only to personal injury cases. It applies to breach of contract cases and defamation cases. It applies to discrimination cases and copyright infringement cases. The test can be used in virtually any situation where someone is contemplating legal action. It can sometimes be easy to identify *merits* and *damages* in a legal matter. But it can sometimes be complex or subtle.

This evaluation of *merits* and *damages* is important because litigation, which is the process of bringing a legal action, can be a costly endeavor. It can be financially costly, in terms of gathering information and researching laws. It can be personally costly, in terms of missing time from work for court appearances. It can be emotionally costly, in terms of the hostile and bitter sentiments that often arise in a lawsuit.

Before learning about how to be a *successful plaintiff*, you'll need to figure out whether or not you want to be a *plaintiff* in the first place. And to do that, you'll need to understand the legal basis of a lawsuit you might be considering. In other words, what is your *cause of action*?

What is a Cause of Action? It's the legal basis of a lawsuit. Being able to recognize a *cause of action* is fundamental to being a successful plaintiff. Here are some of the more commonly pursued causes of action:

Negligence This cause of action hinges on four elements. The first is the existence of a legal duty. The second is a breach of that duty. The third is that someone suffers damages. The fourth is that the breach of the duty caused the damages. Here's an illustration. A bus driver has a legal duty to operate a bus in a safe manner. He exceeds the speed limit, which constitutes a breach of that duty. As a result, he collides with a truck. The collision causes a passenger to fall down and sustain injuries. The collision with the truck is the legal cause of the passenger's injuries, or damages.

Product Liability This cause of action involves SUV rollovers, pharmaceutical drugs, and other product-based matters. It arises when someone is injured by a product which is *defective*. The defect stems from the fact that the product is unreasonably dangerous.

Breach of Contract This cause of action arises when someone fails to perform his duties in a contract. A contract is essentially formed when there is an offer, an acceptance, and no defenses arise as to the formation or enforcement of the contract.

A *cause of action* is the underlying legal theory on which a lawsuit is based. Determining whether a person has a cause of action is sometimes described as the element of, "Do I have a case?"

A good portion of court calendars are filled with lawsuits based on negligence, product liability, professional malpractice, breach of contract, discrimination, harassment, and collection of debts. If I listed all possible causes of action a plaintiff could pursue, this book would have a 40 page appendix. But the commonly arising ones are outlined in the preceding box.

Discrimination is fairly common as a cause of action since it can arise in different settings, such as employment, public access, and education. In the workplace, discrimination takes place when an employer fires, refuses to promote, or refuses to hire someone based on gender, race, nationality, religion, age, pregnancy, or disability. People sometimes confuse sexual discrimination with sexual harassment. The latter is a different cause of action where someone receives unwanted sexual advances.

What Is a Malpractice Lawsuit? We often see advertisements for medical malpractice attorneys who represent plaintiffs injured by hospital or physician errors. Malpractice is essentially a cousin of negligence. The four elements of negligence are applied to the conduct of a professional, such as a physician, attorney, engineer, or financial advisor.

Breach of contract lawsuits can have many forms. Breach of contract typically occurs when someone fails to pay for goods or services received, or fails to perform under the terms of a contract. In the business sector, the fallout of former partners can give rise to various types of lawsuits. These include non-competition clause violations, trademark infringement, and tortious interference with business. Tortious interference occurs when someone intentionally harms the business relationships of another. If former business partners bad-mouth each other, that can result in defamation actions. Defamation consists of false statements that damage someone's reputation. If the false statements are verbal, the cause of action is called slander. If the false statements are written, it's called libel.

There are causes of action based on intellectual property, but these don't often come up with the average person. They include copyright infringement, which is using another's literary or artistic work without permission, or without proper attribution. Trademark infringement occurs when a trademark, such as a company logo or slogan, is improperly used by a competitor or other entity. Patent infringement occurs when someone's invention is used by another without authority or license.

In addition to these traditional causes of action, there are other types of cases, based on workers' compensation, Social Security Disability, and bankruptcy law. Workers' compensation claimants go after wage and medical benefits for on-the-job injuries. In a workers' compensation claim, an employee doesn't need to prove fault on the part of the employer. Simply being injured in the course of employment qualifies someone for these benefits. The workers' compensation system serves to prevent the prosecution of such claims in court. Part of the public policy basis for this is that traditional litigation of such claims would hurt a nation's industries.

In a Social Security Disability case, a claimant files for benefits with the federal government. Claimants must demonstrate a medical condition expected to last at least one year, or result in death. They must also accumulate sufficient *points*, based on years worked. These cases often require reports from doctors or other medical providers to prove there is a physical or mental disability.

In a bankruptcy action, a debtor (person who owes money) asks the court to discharge (wipe away) her debts. The debtor is also called the petitioner. Personal bankruptcy actions are called Chapter 7 bankruptcies, named after the applicable section of the Federal Bankruptcy Code. Filing for bankruptcy stops collection actions while the case is pending in court. If the court decides in favor of the petitioner, debts can be wiped away, depending on income. Although a successful bankruptcy action could stop credit card and hospital bill collectors, it does not eliminate obligations on child support, student loans, and secured loans.

Regardless of the type of action, successful plaintiffs must satisfy all elements of an applicable cause of action. There are good reasons for doing things this way. It enables judges to know what to expect when two adversaries enter a courtroom. Facts may differ. Circumstances may differ. But the general rules for a given cause of action will be legally consistent.

Using the concept of cause of action also enables courts to qualify or disqualify cases in a sensible manner. If a lawsuit is based on product liability, the plaintiff must show one of these three elements to demonstrate that a product was defective:

- The product was defectively manufactured

- The product was defectively designed

- The product failed to carry adequate warnings about its risks

---

The Quick Knockout Punch If a case has merit, a plaintiff can request something called **summary judgment** from the court. *Summary judgment* means there is no dispute as to the facts at hand. The plaintiff asks the court to simply accept the fact that a cause of action exists.

However, it's a double-edged sword, where a defendant can request *summary judgment* to dismiss a plaintiff's case on the grounds that a cause of action does not exist.

If a plaintiff isn't able to satisfy one of these elements, there is no product liability case. If courts didn't force plaintiffs to frame their lawsuits in this manner, our legal system would lack uniformity. Cases would be decided arbitrarily, instead of by standard rules.

The concept of cause of action also enables courts to rely on earlier decisions involving similar cases. This is known as *stare decisis*, which essentially means "to go by something that has already been decided." The more common term we use is *precedent*. This allows courts to compare apples to apples and oranges to oranges.

How to Analyze a Contract in One Minute Breach of contract is one of the most common causes of action in commercial lawsuits. Typical breach of contract cases often involve situations where someone fails to do something, such as *failing to perform services within a given time period, failing to pay for goods that were delivered,* or *failing to deliver goods.* Breach of contract cases can be complex. However, they sometimes hinge upon the issue of whether there was a valid contract in the first place. A simple one-minute analysis can often answer that question.

Was there an **Offer**? Do you want to buy my Volkswagen Jetta?

Was there an **Acceptance**? Yes, I do.

Was there **Consideration**? You give me $4,000 and I'll give you the Jetta.

Did the parties have **Capacity** to enter into a contract? We're both 18, and of sound mind.

Was there a **Meeting of the Minds**? That's the 2005 Jetta in your driveway, right?

Are we free from things (**Defenses**) that would undermine the formation or enforcement of this contract? The odometer hasn't been rolled back. The car isn't stolen.

If you answered "yes" to all these questions, then you probably have a contract. However, keep in mind that this is a very simple contract. In real life, contracts can be complex affairs involving many pages of conditions, clauses, and stipulations.

Let's say a court is faced with a lawsuit that doesn't fit into a clearly definable cause of action. The court will be stuck as to how to proceed. As a result, the court would issue a *demurrer*, which means the lawsuit fails to state a cause of action for which relief (damages) can be granted. A plaintiff doesn't want that to happen.

Formatting lawsuits in this manner serves another purpose. Different causes of action are governed by different *statutes of limitations*, which are time periods within which legal actions must be brought. After a statute of limitations expires, a case is dead. It doesn't matter that the wrongdoer was seen drinking all night long at a bar before he got into his car. It doesn't matter that five credible eyewitnesses saw him jump a divider and smash head-on into the victim's car. If the statute of limitations expires, the matter is forever dead.

There's a public policy reason for enforcing statutes of limitations. Without them, the right to bring lawsuits could linger indefinitely. Courts could be bogged down with cases that were decades old, where witnesses had died, laws had changed, or where it simply wouldn't be fair to hold someone accountable after so much time had passed. For obvious reasons, the concept doesn't apply to serious crimes. There is no statute of limitations for dragging a murderer out of the woodwork. It's worth noting that statutes of limitations can differ from state to state.

Let's back up a little to the business about the *merit* of a legal matter. I said the successful plaintiff looks to see if her case has *merit*. It seems like a simple enough rule to follow. But you'd be surprised how many plaintiffs (not successful ones) initiate cases that *don't* have merit. These people aren't stupid. They aren't ignorant. Why then do they initiate such lawsuits? They initiate them for the *wrong reasons*.

Successful plaintiffs *do not* bring legal actions for the *wrong reasons*. What does that mean? It means successful plaintiffs don't sue people because they are *angry* at them. They don't sue people because they *hate* them. They don't sue people to *get even* with them. Successful plaintiffs only start a legal battle when there is a valid cause of action that has merit and there is a prize to be obtained in the end.

A lawsuit brought for irrational reasons is a textbook example of picking the wrong battle. The consequences can be unnecessary expense and aggravation. The consequences can include penalties for abusing the legal process, or allegations of bringing a frivolous lawsuit.

What is the lesson of this chapter? A successful plaintiff picks battles carefully. There must be a valid legal basis for a lawsuit (merit) and something worthwhile to pursue (damages). A successful plaintiff determines if her legal matter fits into a valid cause of action.

The Successful Plaintiff Exploits an Adversary's Weaknesses

"The clever combatant imposes his will on the enemy, but does not allow the enemy's will be to be imposed on him."

Sun Tzu, *The Art of War*

There's a well known military treatise called *The Art of War*. It was written by the Chinese strategist Sun Tzu in the 6th Century B.C. In its day, it was the seminal work on how to wage war. Despite the advent of million dollar cruise missiles that can be programmed to fly down an enemy's chimney, the philosophy of Sun Tzu is still respected in military circles.

Tactics have changed. Technology has changed. But the basic philosophies of how to fight a military battle have not. And a military battle shares similarities with a legal battle. A legal battle may not involve deadly weapons, but it involves strategies and tactics. A legal battle involves planning. It involves gathering information about an opponent. It involves identifying an opponent's strengths and figuring out the most effective ways to neutralize their threat.

Sun Tzu understood the need to exploit the weaknesses of an enemy. Likewise, a successful plaintiff identifies weaknesses in a legal adversary's position. You might say this is common sense. But you'd be surprised how many plaintiffs fail to do this. That's because they're too busy concentrating on an offensive plan. This omission can be dangerous because an adversary will be searching for weaknesses in your case. And if you're facing a large firm and the stakes are high, your case will be scrutinized with a magnifying glass at enemy headquarters.

The most fundamental weakness your adversary will examine is whether you've met the elements of a valid cause of action. A legal *cause of action* is like a jigsaw puzzle made up of three, four, or five elements. Take away one of those elements and there is no lawsuit. Let's say a speeding motorist is talking on his cell phone and nearly causes an accident. No one is hurt and nothing is damaged. Although the motorist committed a *breach of duty* to operate a car in a safe manner, there is no *cause of action* for negligence if there are no *damages*.

A defendant would love nothing more than to have a plaintiff's case dismissed because it fails to state a *cause of action*. Well, actually there is one other thing a defendant really loves, which is to have a case dismissed because the *statute of limitations* has expired. But from the previous chapter, readers can appreciate how a successful plaintiff will avoid making either of these fundamental mistakes.

Your adversary's position may contain a weakness in the form of a *conflict*. We recognize the term *conflict* to mean war or fighting. But in a legal context, conflict means something slightly different. It means someone is doing something which is ethically at odds with his other existing duties. The more correct term for the concept is *conflict of interest*, but most attorneys simply use the term *conflict*.

Conflicts can arise in any legal setting. Picture this scenario. It can be improper for an attorney to represent both seller and buyer in the same real estate transaction. The interests of the seller are invariably at odds with the interests of the buyer. This can be illustrated with the sale of a house. Let's say the buyer wants the seller to repair leaks in the roof. These repairs would cost the seller $2,000. Look at what happens when an attorney represents both parties. If the attorney recommends roof repairs, he shortchanges the seller. If he doesn't recommend roof repairs, he shortchanges the buyer. Our attorney can't protect one party in this transaction without compromising the interests of the other.

Conflicts can arise in many legal settings. Some are more obvious than others. Could an attorney simultaneously represent the interests of both husband and wife in a divorce? The answer is no. One spouse may want $3,000 a month in maintenance, while the other insists on paying only $2,000 a month. That's an easy conflict to identify. But you might say, "Wait a minute… I see those divorce mediation attorneys who bring both spouses to the table. Isn't that a conflict?" No, it isn't, because the role of a mediator is different than that of an attorney providing exclusive representation to only one spouse.

Isn't It My Attorney's Job to Identify My Adversary's Weaknesses? That's a good point. If you place yourself in the hands of a competent attorney, she would be the one looking for legal conflicts, improprieties, misconduct, and other such weaknesses in your adversary's position. But not all plaintiffs choose to retain an attorney. For them, this is important material. And even when a plaintiff retains an attorney, this is still important.

Think of it this way. When you go to a doctor, you don't simply sit down at the examination table and say, "Doc, please figure out what's wrong with me." You tell the doctor about all your aches and pains. You're careful to describe whether the pains are sharp, localized, or dull. You're careful to describe the times of day when you feel the pains and the things you suspect of bringing them on. You tell your doctor about your diet and your personal habits, such as exercise. You tell your doctor about medications you take. You provide as much detailed information as possible so that your doctor can formulate the best diagnosis.

Just the same, a successful plaintiff advises his attorney about all the things done to him by the other side. The attorney analyzes the legal ramifications of those things. A successful plaintiff looks back on his own "patient history" and shares his observations with his attorney. That's why it's important for all plaintiffs to understand these issues, whether they retain attorneys or represent themselves.

Not all situations involving *conflicts* are as simple to identify. Here's a zinger out of left field. Is there a conflict between an attorney and his client in a personal injury lawsuit? Your gut reaction is probably that there isn't. An attorney represents the injured client against a negligent defendant.

They're on the same team. There's no conflict there. It seems straightforward enough.

But wait! Some legal scholars argue that isn't the case. They say there's an inherent conflict here because an attorney often wants a case to be settled without excessive effort. The attorney wants his fee sooner than later. And he wants this fee without a costly trial. This is arguably at odds with the notion that a client is entitled to the maximum money award, which can often require a costly trial.

An astute observer can identify conflicts where they might not be readily apparent. Conflicts are generally addressed in rules of professional conduct and ethics, as well as rules of evidence. Learning to identify them is not merely an academic exercise for a law school class. It's real life and it's important. Picture this scenario:

Samuel is a 48 year old administrative assistant. The school district is trying to fire him, alleging that his work performance is unsatisfactory. Samuel argues that his performance for the past ten years has been better than satisfactory. He insists the school district is committing age discrimination against him. The school district offers statements from Samuel's co-worker, another administrative assistant, who says Samuel regularly makes mistakes entering data, and is uncooperative about correcting his work. Samuel objects that such testimony is biased because both Samuel and the other administrative assistant applied for the same supervisor position last month. Samuel argues that the administrative assistant would say just about anything to eliminate competition for the position. This is a good identification of a conflict by Samuel.

Another weakness to look for in your adversary's position is the existence of an *impropriety*, or the *appearance of an impropriety*. An *impropriety* is something ethically wrong that your adversary did. Here's something to think about in this vein. In recent years, many cities and towns have installed traffic cameras to catch motorists going through red lights. My theory is that the rapid proliferation of these cameras means local governments have become deeply concerned about our safety. But some people say my theory is wrong. They say these cities and towns don't give a rat's tail about our safety. They say some of these cities and towns are even going so far as reducing the duration of the yellow light in the green-yellow-red sequence, simply because they WANT motorists to get ticketed.

I have trouble believing that, because it would mean these cities and towns are committing *improprieties*. I reassure myself that these traffic cameras are out there for only one purpose, which is to protect the SAFETY of the public. But if my theory was wrong, and the towns were ramping down the yellow light times, I suppose that would be a good example of an *impropriety*.

The *appearance of impropriety* is something a little different, but still useful to a plaintiff. It's when someone hasn't exactly done anything wrong, but the appearance of a situation doesn't exactly cast them in a good light. You might hear the term used by politicians who are fastidious about their public image, where they'll tell their staffs, "I don't even want the *appearance* of impropriety here."

What is the Statute of Frauds? It's a rule that requires certain contracts to be in writing. In general, a contract doesn't need to be in writing to be enforceable. However, certain contracts are considered special and must be in writing. These are:

- contracts for the sale of goods of $500 or more

- contracts transferring real property interests

- contracts for paying the debt of another person

- contracts where performance can't be completed within one year

- prenuptial agreements and agreements made in consideration of marriage

- certain contracts for executors in an estate

Here's an example of the appearance of an impropriety. Let's say a politician proposes a law that will require public schools to include whole grain foods in cafeteria lunches. It sounds like a good plan. But let's say the politician's husband is a manager at a local whole grain foods company. It would be difficult to say whether the husband stands to benefit directly from the law proposed by his wife. But think about the appearance of the situation. It doesn't look good. This is what's meant by the appearance of an impropriety.

Did your adversary commit a *crime*? This may sound absurd because the notion of a crime brings to mind the image of bungling bank robbers shooting at cops in a high-speed car chase. However, we live in a world where certain types of conduct are increasingly becoming criminalized. What does the word *criminalized* mean? That's a 50¢ legal term in itself. It means that wrongful conduct which society once treated as a civil violation has now become a crime.

Perhaps one of the most recognizable examples of criminalized conduct is *driving while intoxicated*. There was a time when people drank all night long at parties and then got in their cars to drive home. Sometimes they made it home in one piece without injuring anyone, and sometimes they didn't. Throughout the nation, social outrage grew towards such inexcusable conduct. Organizations emerged and got the message across that drunk driving was more than just a social folly. It was grossly irresponsible and potentially deadly conduct that called for serious punishment. As a result, the nation started to treat drunk driving as a crime.

The concept of criminalization has permeated into other areas of our society. If a ship ran aground during the 1950s and oil spilled onto tourist beaches, the ship's navigation officers would face disciplinary action from their corporate office. Today, they could face jail sentences under a myriad of federal environmental laws that make the act of spilling oil onto navigable waters a crime. If your adversary's conduct amounts to a crime, that's something you need to explore as a plaintiff.

In order for your adversary's conduct to be considered a crime, it must satisfy a basic two-part test. The test asks (1.) if the person committed a criminal act, and (2.) if the person had the requisite mental state. A criminal act is conduct which is prohibited by society. Physically assaulting someone, killing someone, stealing someone's property, threatening someone, breaking into someone's home... these are all *criminal acts*.

The second element, *mental state*, is the more complex part of this test. To be considered a criminal, the suspect's mental state must fit into one of four categories. These are *(i.) intentionally, (ii.) knowingly, (iii.) recklessly,* or *(iv.) with criminal negligence*. In some states, penal codes don't use these exact words. However, they apply the same basic idea. When a person acts *intentionally*, he acts voluntarily and deliberately in carrying out an act. If he breaks into a business rival's store with a five gallon jug of gasoline and a lighter in the middle of the night, he demonstrates his *intentional* state of mind to commit arson.

If a criminal acts *knowingly*, it means she commits an act where she is reasonably certain of its consequences. For instance, if someone lights a pack of firecrackers and throws it down from the nosebleed section of a sports stadium, she should have no delusions about the consequences of her actions. She could turn to a friend sitting next to her and say, "I hope those firecrackers don't land on anyone because it isn't my intention to injure anyone." That absurd statement wouldn't serve to lessen her guilt. If anything, it would only irritate jurors.

If a criminal acts *recklessly*, it means he realizes his actions jeopardize others, but chooses to act in such a manner anyway. A good example is a pilot of a small airplane flying at low altitude over the water to buzz and scare boaters. He does this to impress his friends in the plane. He recognizes the risk created by his irresponsible conduct, yet chooses to ignore it.

The test for *criminal negligence* is similar to the test for *recklessness*. However, with criminal negligence, the wrongdoer *doesn't* recognize the risk created by his conduct. Let's say a factory supervisor allows a repair contractor to enter an empty gasoline storage tank to perform repairs. The supervisor isn't aware of combustible vapors in the tank. When the contractor lights off his oxy-acetylene torch, it ignites the vapors and he suffers burns. If the contractor brings a lawsuit for his injuries, he'll bring up the *criminal negligence* of the supervisor's conduct.

It's unlikely your opponent will have committed a crime. But you might be surprised. Leaving the scene of accident as a motorist can be a crime. Writing a bad check can be a crime. Using the postal system to engage in fraudulent or other questionable acts can be a crime. Sometimes it's a matter of being alert enough to realize your adversary committed a crime, even if it's only a misdemeanor.

There Once Was a Time When Plaintiffs Didn't Stand a Chance In the 1800s, the United States and Europe made tremendous industrial strides. The advent of steam engines and modern manufacturing techniques resulted in explosive economic growth. Men made fortunes in steel, shipbuilding, and railroads. However, the ordinary person worked long workdays in dangerous factories, with slim chances for a comfortable and dignified retirement. The legal system of the day protected wealthy industrialists more than the children who labored in their textile mills. During these bleak days, there lived an ugly three-headed monster that slaughtered plaintiffs who were naive enough to believe they could challenge this system in court. This "monster" was made up of these three legal concepts:

Privity of Contract Only parties to a contract had the right to sue a manufacturer on the contract. Consumers were not considered parties to a contract. This concept was used to dismiss lawsuits of plaintiffs injured by dangerous cars and other products.

Contributory Negligence If a plaintiff was responsible for his injuries, even as little as 1%, he was totally barred from recovery against the wrongdoer.

Assumption of Risk Plaintiffs assumed the risk associated with an activity when they engaged in the activity.

At this point, you might think you've learned a lot about how to take the wind out of an adversary's sails. But here's a quick reality check. Just as you're looking for weaknesses in your adversary's armor, he's looking for weaknesses in yours. Sun Tzu's treatise advises that strategic opportunities should be recognized, and that opportunities should not be created for the enemy. The successful plaintiff takes steps to eliminate weaknesses in his case, or at least reduce their impact.

In addition to conflicts, improprieties, crimes, or other wrongful acts, a defendant will try to show that your *own* conduct contributed to your damages. Maybe you failed to take steps to lessen your damages. Maybe you used a product improperly. Maybe you failed to do something you were supposed to do, such as fastening your seatbelt. If you're in a comparative negligence jurisdiction, the damages to which you would otherwise be entitled are offset by your share of blame in the matter.

Another weakness is *fraud*. This means you acted in a manner that misled and deceived the other side. Did you make *representations*, either innocently or knowingly? Depending on their severity, an adversary could argue that such things should prevent you from being allowed to enforce a contract. The *clean hands doctrine* asks if your own hands were "clean" in your dealings with the other side. Did your conduct amount to "dirty pool" or did you act honorably?

If the damages you're demanding in a commercial lawsuit are excessive, your adversary could argue you shouldn't be rewarded with such *unjust enrichment*. If your conduct was outrageous enough to shock the sensibilities of a normal person, an adversary could argue that it would be *unconscionable* to rule in your favor. However, it's a two-way street, meaning that these concepts can be used by both sides in a lawsuit.

Whether your lawsuit involves personal injury, divorce, breach of contract, or stockbroker fraud, there are things you may have done that provide your adversary with defenses against you. In legal terms, these *things* are called *affirmative defenses*. They arise in federal and state rules of civil procedure. Some of these *things* you have no control over, but some of them you do.

Below are some commonly arising affirmative defenses. Keep in mind this list is general in nature.

▪ Accord and satisfaction - You and your adversary reached an agreement.

▪ Assumption of risk - You knowingly engaged in conduct that caused your injuries.

▪ Authority - Your adversary had authority to do what he did.

▪ Consent - Your adversary had consent to do what he did.

▪ Duress - Undue pressure was exerted against your adversary, such as threats.

▪ Estoppel - Your adversary acted in reliance upon something you did or said.

▪ Contributory Negligence - Your conduct contributed to your injuries.

Affirmative defenses - continued:

• State of Frauds - The contract had to be in writing.

• Statute of Limitations - Your action was not filed within the required time period.

• Waiver - You waived your rights.

• Release - You released your adversary from further liability or obligation.

There are other defenses as well, some of which are specific to particular types of lawsuits. Readers should be aware that this outline of legal defenses is general in nature, and not meant to be an exhaustive list.

What is the lesson of this chapter? A successful plaintiff looks for weaknesses in an adversary's legal position, while at the same time making efforts to reduce her own weaknesses.

The Successful Plaintiff Possesses a Plaintiff's Attitude

"The test of a first-rate intelligence is the ability to hold two opposed ideas in the mind at the same time, and still retain the ability to function. One should, for example, be able to see that things are hopeless and yet be determined to make them otherwise."

F. Scott Fitzgerald

Attitude is a very important factor in life. Needless to say, it's a very important aspect of being a successful plaintiff. Attitude is a favorite subject of football coaches, motivational speakers, and super-achievers in the business world. Life isn't strictly about IQ scores, physical ability, or artistic talent. It's about having the attitude to do the best with what you have.

People spend thousands of dollars to acquire that elusive thing we call a "winning attitude." They attend seminars and read books. They walk over beds of hot coals in motivational exercises. They travel to far ends of the world to be touched by the wisdom of spiritual leaders. They listen to audio tapes in their cars, hoping to learn some secret, or some insight, to help break the shackles holding them back from greatness.

With all these efforts, people come to realize that achieving success ultimately comes down to one's outlook on life. It isn't necessarily about having an MBA from a prestigious business school. Thousands of people have those. It isn't necessarily about having a trust fund from an uncle who made a fortune on Wall Street.

It helps to have such things in life. But on a more fundamental level, it's about *attitude*. If that wasn't the case, there would be no explaining why so many brilliant and highly educated people have trouble paying their rent, while entrepreneurs who never went to college sometimes have trouble figuring out what to do with their millions. Sure, luck can be a factor in all things. But *attitude* is a major factor, both in life and in legal matters.

In legal matters, there are a number of ways in which attitude enters the equation. Part of a successful plaintiff's attitude lies in believing that a legal matter can be won. There have always been cases in legal history that seemed hopeless. Yet the plaintiffs didn't throw their hands up in despair. Sometimes, it's simply a matter of seeing a glass of water as half full instead of half empty. Every legal situation has its strong points and weak points. A successful plaintiff weighs both and figures out ways to move forward.

A successful plaintiff also adopts the attitude that he deserves to win. He enters the fray with strong conviction. If it's monetary compensation he's suing for, he rationalizes his right to a large award. He was wronged and the wrongdoer is going to pay for it. If the wrongdoer cannot pay for it, he will look to see who else can be held accountable, by virtue of a relationship with the wrongdoer.

This is why we often see multiple defendants named in lawsuits. If the lawsuit is based on a dangerous product, the plaintiff may name the designer, manufacturer, distributor, retailer, or other entities as defendants. This attribute of the successful plaintiff has been a source of criticism for our legal system. That's because defendants with "deep pockets" can be unfairly targeted, for no other reason than the fact that they present the only viable source of money for a plaintiff.

The successful plaintiff is decisive. In contrast, there are plaintiffs who defeat their lawsuits before they even begin, by giving things too much thought. They ask themselves whether they're doing the right thing by becoming plaintiffs. They ask themselves if they want to spend years fighting in court. They ask themselves what their friends will think of them for suing another person. The successful plaintiff doesn't think about issues on such a deep level. The successful plaintiff is a "damn the torpedoes, full speed ahead" type of person.

Successful plaintiffs tend to be ambitious and aggressive. A lawsuit is an endeavor that takes effort. Things don't just happen by themselves. A lawsuit takes preparation, research, and determination. An important lawsuit is comparable to other major campaigns in a person's life. Like the application process for college, lawsuits involve lots of repetitive and tedious paperwork. Like the interview process for an important job, they take rehearsal and showmanship.

Successful plaintiffs tend to be awake and alert. They don't hit the *snooze* button in life. They behave proactively towards adversities that life throws at them. They tend to be effective communicators who aren't on the shy side. They aren't intimidated by personal interaction and they liberally use telephones, e-mails, and text messaging to stay on top of their affairs. They avoid ambiguity in their personal and business communications. They take prompt action in directly confronting problems. As such, they avoid becoming defendants in other people's lawsuits. But in the role of plaintiff, they do a good job of articulating the wrongs done to them.

Successful plaintiffs are confident. They trust their abilities to accomplish things. They don't ask permission to do the things they do. They reach out and take what they believe should be theirs. If their actions draw criticism, they simply step back and ask forgiveness. They don't let others get in their way. They are competitive in spirit, looking at a legal endeavor as a contest. They assess the people, laws, and social mechanisms that stand in their way. And they formulate plans to defeat such obstacles.

Successful plaintiffs exhibit high levels of self-worth and assertiveness. No one is going to push them around or trample their rights. They don't have little voices in their heads that tell them, "Oh, come on! You're not going to really sue that store because their guard politely asked you to open your shopping bag, are you? Did you really suffer humiliation and mental distress by that brief detainment? The security guard was only doing her job, and she was courteous in the way she did it." The successful plaintiff can put aside her forgiving tendencies. She will more likely say, "That guard had no right to do that to me! I'm a customer in this store, not a trespasser. I deserve to be treated with dignity. I was violated!" If need be, she'll break into tears.

The Bursting Real Estate Bubble Several years ago, the real estate market looked like there was no end in sight for home prices. It was like a feeding frenzy, where people were given all sorts of incentives to become first-time home buyers. Some buyers shouldn't have bought the homes they did, because their mortgages were written on thin ice.

But what happened? The real estate market crashed. Home owners weren't able to keep up with their mortgage payments, and they faced foreclosure. This wasn't part of the plan. Instead of complacently entering the role of defaulting debtor, some home buyers became plaintiffs, arguing that they were given mortgages that shouldn't have been given to them. Some prevailed and got to keep their homes.

That's because they had the attitude to seize the situation and conduct themselves as *successful plaintiffs* instead of *unsuccessful debtors*.

I'm not saying successful plaintiffs are good human beings or bad human beings. They simply tend to possess an attitude that enables them to excel in the role of plaintiff. Whether such an attitude endears them to the general public is a different matter. But successful plaintiffs aren't usually overly concerned about what others would think. They often have single-minded focus on a lawsuit. They don't allow obstacles to get in the way of succeeding in a lawsuit.

Successful plaintiffs aren't likely to feel pangs of guilt over the effects of their lawsuits on society. In other words, successful plaintiffs are generally not *altruists*. An *altruist* is someone who puts the interests of others before his own interests. Successful plaintiffs don't generally reflect, "Oh gosh, I can't do that. If everyone sued for what I'm suing for, what would this world come to?"

You might ask, "What about those plaintiffs who hold press conferences to announce that their lawsuits aren't about money, but more about making sure that what happened to them doesn't happen to someone else. Isn't that being altruistic and selfless?" It can be, but many of those people usually don't mind cashing a six-figure settlement check when the dust settles. Yes, some of them ARE genuinely interested in making sure others don't go through what they went through. But others may simply want to come off looking good in a situation where they stand to make out well financially. And some of them keenly appreciate how a good press conference can impart energy to a lawsuit.

But going back to altruism, think of the institution of bankruptcy. The plaintiff, called a petitioner in this context, asks the bankruptcy court to relieve him of his debts. This person doesn't tell himself, "You can't do that. If everyone in your position did that, what would happen to the banks and lending institutions?" An old-fashioned type of person might think, "You borrowed that money and you're going to pay it back. You're going to take a second job. You're going to skip buying that morning coffee and you're going to make good to those people."

In contrast, a successful plaintiff identifies reasons why he is entitled to have his debts forgiven. HE is the one who was wronged. The banks shouldn't have thrown credit cards at him. The lending institutions should have known HE wouldn't be able to keep up with that aggressive ten year mortgage. It wasn't his fault the loans became overwhelming. It wasn't his fault his business went under and he couldn't pay back his creditors. A successful plaintiff convinces himself that HE is the victim!

The successful plaintiff tells himself that multimillion dollar corporations use bankruptcy laws to get out of bad business situations every day, only to open up shop under new names six months later. Why shouldn't these same bankruptcy laws protect the little guy who's in a REAL financial rut? The successful plaintiff rationalizes things in ways that justify his actions.

He tells himself that corporations in the United States are screwing the American people left and right. They're sending their manufacturing overseas to third world countries where labor is dirt cheap. They're reaping unprecedented profits. If things don't go as planned, they file for bankruptcy and start over again. They're screwing Uncle Sam's tax collectors by keeping their money offshore. He asks himself, "Why should I, as an $11/hour associate at a toy store, be overly concerned about the impact of my bankruptcy case on the nation as a whole?" People can justify many things in their minds, among the easiest of which may be entering the role of plaintiff.

After reading this, some might say that this quality which I describe as *attitude* contains elements of *self-entitlement*. That argument could be made, but the successful plaintiff convinces himself he deserves to be compensated for his troubles. Successful plaintiffs don't look at every intellectual argument that can be made for or against them. They do what they have to do to take care of number one.

Another important aspect of the attitudes of successful plaintiffs is that they are fighters. They aren't easily intimidated and don't back down if there's a valid reason to stand fast. Our legal system favors the fighter, sometimes even when the fighter isn't always right. The plaintiff who comes out swinging and puts the adversary on the ropes enjoys an advantage. In fact, this is an aspect of our society which is criticized by legal scholars. They point out that in other countries, unsuccessful plaintiffs must reimburse defendants for the cost of defending a lawsuit.

Successful plaintiffs are not easily intimidated into backing down from a fight. Consider a workplace scenario where a mechanic vehemently objects to performing a task she claims is unsafe. The setting is an industrial plant where she is ordered to climb a ladder to inspect a motor in a precariously high location. She insists on having a safety person present. Union rules call for a safety person, but the bad economy has resulted in management flexing its muscles with increasing regularity.

The Bankruptcy Reform Act of 2005 Wiping away your debts by filing for bankruptcy is not as easy as it used to be. Chapter 7 bankruptcy, traditionally used by individuals to make their financial obligations vanish, doesn't work the way it used to. In April 2005, President George Bush signed the Bankruptcy Reform Act, which imposed new conditions, some of which are listed below:

- Debtors whose income is above the median income for their state (and who would be able to repay $5,000 of their debts over a period of five years) have to make arrangements for a repayment plan instead of simply having their debts eliminated.

- Debtors need to participate in credit counseling.

- Homestead exemptions can be capped at $125,000.

- Purchases of $500 or more made within 90 days of filing for bankruptcy have to be paid back.

The supervisor tells her, "Get up on that ladder and inspect the oil level in that motor. I'm short two people tonight and the last thing I need now is your attitude." In such a situation, many people would obediently follow the supervisor's orders. But this mechanic insists on having a safety person present, or else she'll call a shop steward. This makes the supervisor think twice about dealing with a grievance. This employee isn't objecting to taking out a bag of garbage. She's standing her ground on what presents itself to be a valid safety issue.

The supervisor realizes the old intimidation tactic isn't working here. If the situation blows out of proportion, it could look like management's violation of safety protocols. The employee's position is a valid one, but many people wouldn't have her bold attitude to stand her ground.

Pride does not suppress the attitude of the successful plaintiff. Pride is a human trait that some see as a sign of weakness and some see as a sign of character. Pride prevents people from doing things they may wish to do, but feel shameful in doing. "Boys don't cry," is a good example of how the trait of pride has permeated into social norms. But successful plaintiffs aren't inhibited in this regard. "It hurts when I raise my arm. I'm not able to carry those tools for eight hours." Those are things a successful plaintiff isn't ashamed to say. This brings one to the realization that while the law tends to be a logical and analytical subject, the attitude of a plaintiff can be a somewhat emotional subject.

Attitude is a big part of life. And after reading this chapter, one realizes it's a big part of being a successful plaintiff. The successful plaintiff's attitude has many facets. It can be a conviction that she deserves to win. It can be the courage not to back down. It can be the ability to see a positive outcome for a matter that appears hopeless. These attitudes do not necessarily make a plaintiff a better or worse human being. These attitudes enable a plaintiff to get through the adversity and uncertainty of a lawsuit.

What is the lesson of this chapter? A successful plaintiff embodies an attitude that energizes her through a lawsuit. She does not lose momentum by having doubts or reservations about her actions. She is single-minded and goal-oriented in her legal endeavor.

Tamara Kismet

The Successful Plaintiff Chooses a Good Attorney, if Necessary

"Well, I don't know as I want a lawyer to tell me what I cannot do. I hire him to tell me how to do what I want to do."

J. Pierpont Morgan

There may come a time in a legal matter when a plaintiff needs to think about retaining a good attorney. In some instances, this can be at the very start. In others, it can be two years into a lawsuit. It all depends on the plaintiff and the situation. There are plaintiffs who choose to remain at the helm of their legal affairs without ever bringing an attorney into the picture.

But if a plaintiff does need to select an attorney, it can be one of the most important decisions in a legal matter. It can also be one of the most difficult decisions to make. One of the reasons for this is society's natural mistrust and animosity towards attorneys. Centuries ago, William Shakespeare wrote the play *Henry VI*, which contained the line, "The first thing we do, let's kill all the lawyers."

Shakespeare's immortal line goes to show that attorneys were hated even in the 16th century. It isn't difficult to dislike attorneys. Collectively characterized as vultures, thieves, scoundrels, and bloodsuckers, few professionals are vilified as much as attorneys. It's a shame, because there are many attorneys out there who are decent human beings. They help those who can't help themselves against an unjust system. Not all attorneys are rich. Not all attorneys fleece old widows out of their estates. As with any professional, there are good attorneys and bad ones.

There is no law that says a plaintiff must be represented by an attorney. A plaintiff who hires an attorney becomes a *client*. A plaintiff who flies solo without an attorney becomes a *pro se* plaintiff. The decision to handle your own legal matter is an important one that should be given serious thought. On one hand, you're looking at the arduous job of preparing your own legal documents, conducting your own research, and handling your own court appearances. It can be an intimidating endeavor, although not as daunting as it was thirty years ago.

Today, many companies sell legal forms and assist customers in filling them out. There are many resources on the internet that non-attorneys can use to research statutes and court decisions. Handling your own case can mean walking away with thousands more in your pocket, but it can also mean wondering if you would have obtained even more if a good attorney had represented you.

Some *pro se* plaintiffs look forward to the educational experience that comes with handling their own lawsuits. And as much as it's difficult for attorneys to admit, a plaintiff who appears in court without high-priced legal counsel can sometimes earn the respect and admiration of a judge. But that can depend on the judge and the situation. Some judges could be annoyed by the idea of a plaintiff stumbling and bumbling through a trial, at great inconvenience and expense to a county court system, all for the purpose of saving a few bucks.

Not All Attorneys Charge $500 an Hour People sometimes find it intimidating to approach an attorney for a consultation. It may be because paralegals or secretaries usually screens calls in most law offices. Law firms operate like this because their attorneys would never get any work done if they personally spoke with every caller. Although the process may seem distancing, don't forget that attorneys ultimately need clients to pay the bills.

Some court systems are tailored for the pro se plaintiff. In small claims court, many plaintiffs appear without attorneys. However, there can be limitations on the types of cases brought in small claims court. In addition, small claims court will only preside over relatively small cases, where the amount in dispute doesn't exceed several thousand dollars. One of the nice things about the internet is that many court systems offer extensive online resources, such as blank forms and other helpful documents. The more time you leave yourself with applicable deadlines, the more time you'll have to leisurely explore your options.

If you decide that going it alone isn't worth the trouble or the risk, you'll need to find a good attorney. That decision must be made using both your head and your heart. That's because your attorney should be knowledgeable and experienced, and at the same time, have a personality you can work with. If you don't click from the start, it could be a sign that this isn't a person with whom you'd like to discuss personal and confidential matters. Some lawsuits take years to resolve, meaning that you and your attorney might have to work closely for the long haul.

Why Do People Sue? The answer to that question could fill a book in itself! But for our purposes, we'll be practical. In general, people sue to enforce their rights. The rights often involve money compensation for damages or injuries. But people sue for many other reasons, such as forcing a school district to implement a curriculum, forcing a contractor to halt construction, forcing a government agency to release information, or forcing someone to perform under the terms of a contract.

The aim of many civil lawsuits is to obtain money as a form of compensation for a wrong. The wrong might be an engineering firm's design error that resulted in a bridge collapse. The wrong might be a company's failure to pay for office supplies. Our legal system uses money as a means of compensating people for the wrongs they suffered at the hands of others.

Although law has always been considered an elite profession, legal services have become more affordable in recent decades. The self-help legal industry has expanded tremendously, offering plaintiffs excellent resources for handling their matters pro se. Another factor driving down the cost of legal services is that there are more attorneys out there than there used to be. The nation's law schools continue to churn out thousands of graduates every year. However, good legal jobs have not been growing at the same pace. There are bright associates at the top of the class who make $120,000 a year right out of school.

How Do Attorneys Set Their Fees? Understanding how attorneys charge for services can help you obtain the information you need for the *most reasonable* price. There are several ways attorneys charge for legal services. There are *flat fee* arrangements. This is where you retain an attorney to handle a real estate closing or personal bankruptcy at a flat fee, say $1,400. You won't pay a penny more, even if the attorney loses considerable time in clearing up headaches with non-working appliances, tax arrears, and liens on a house.

Attorneys also charge clients on an *hourly fee* basis, just like an auto repair shop. This is the way most divorce or criminal cases are handled. If the attorney charges $250 per hour, she may tell the client, "I need a $7,500 retainer to get started on your case." The retainer will cover thirty hours of work. In accident cases, attorneys work on a *contingency fee* basis. This means the attorney fee is generally one third of all money won in a lawsuit, after deducting court costs and other expenses. If an attorney accepts a case on this basis, he must obtain a favorable verdict or settlement. Otherwise, he doesn't get paid a dime.

Don't be shy about asking an attorney about fee arrangements. If you're contemplating a lawsuit in connection with an accident, dangerous product, or medical malpractice matter, the consultation shouldn't cost you anything. If the legal matter involves something else, an attorney may still give you a 10 minute consultation for free... simply to figure out if he wants to represent you.

But jobs at that level are few and far between. Some readers may remember how books and films during the '80s and '90s depicted the legal profession as a world of privilege and power. Much has changed since those days. Like many other industries, the legal field has not been immune to the laws of supply and demand. Although this is bad news for students preparing for their law school admission tests, it's good news for plaintiffs looking to hire an attorney.

One way to pick an attorney is to open up the Yellow Pages and go down the list, starting with the letter "A" and working your way through the alphabet. Although this may seem comical today, it's the way many people searched for legal services in the past. But with the internet, everything has changed.

The internet is obviously the most powerful tool for finding an attorney nowadays. You can choose from a number of online legal databases that list attorneys by various parameters. You can search for an attorney based on the size of the law firm, area of practice, geographic location, or law school attended. If it matters to you, you can even see an attorney's photo after following links to the law firm's website.

Some people don't use online databases. They simply go to a web browser and type in what they're looking for, such as *personal injury attorney los angeles*, or *divorce lawyer philadelphia*. Performing a search this way can also be productive. Just keep in mind that not all attorneys are able to market themselves aggressively on the internet. There are tons of good attorneys who are simply too busy to develop a web presence. It takes considerable time and money for a law firm to get itself to appear in the first few pages of an internet search.

Big Law Firm versus Small Law Firm Does selecting a small law firm give you a better deal for your money than a large law firm? It can depend on the nature of the legal matter you have. People tend to think that a large law firm brings them the highest quality legal services. That can be the case, but firms of every size today work hard to deliver quality.

This is simply because lots of attorneys out there are hustling for the same finite pool of clients. Newly graduated attorneys who become frustrated with the bleak job market sometimes set up shop right out of law school. This increases competition among firms of all sizes. Smaller firms often promise more personal service and accessibility than large firms. But larger firms can be more powerful in terms of their influence and reputation.

In certain types of lawsuits, having a heavy hitter in your corner can be an important factor. A large and powerful firm can sometimes leverage better terms in a lawsuit than a small firm because adversaries realize large firms have the horsepower for a long court battle. But every case is different. It really depends on the firm, the geographic region, the density of attorneys in the area, the nature of the legal matter, and ultimately... your personal preference. Many people select an attorney based on recommendations from family members or professional colleagues.

The best thing to do is to explore the opinions of friends and colleagues, research firms on your own, and pay attention to your gut feelings.

Finding a good attorney can take time because the process can involve speaking with several attorneys before making a decision. And it's a complex decision. Everyone wants an advocate who is knowledgeable and experienced.

In the very least, an attorney should be competent, reasonably priced, adequately personable, and geographically practical. People don't usually select an attorney by looking at a roadmap. However, geography is a consideration. After all, there's no point in driving two hours to appear for a deposition at a law firm located 100 miles from your home.

It's funny that plaintiffs will sometimes base their decisions on attributes that are highly personal, such as an attorney's demeanor, attitude, courtesy, physical appearance, attentiveness, or even sense of humor. It is, after all, a highly personal decision. In a brief telephone conversation, a client may not be able to delve into an attorney's detailed knowledge of a legal subject. However, a client could form an opinion as to whether the attorney is organized, quick-witted, or condescending.

In hiring an attorney, a plaintiff is often forced to make the best possible decision with only a minimal level of information. A fifteen minute free consultation may offer a glimpse into the attorney's basic knowledge and personality, but it may not shed light on other attributes. Will the attorney will be attentive in returning phone calls? Will the attorney be petty in charging for every little fax and photocopy? Will the attorney put your interests above all else, including his own interests? Will the attorney always be "in court" when you call his office?

These are things a plaintiff may only learn about after signing on the dotted line. However, if it turns out that the match wasn't a good one, the relationship isn't cast in stone. A plaintiff can change attorneys without restriction. If that happens, the attorney must generally be compensated for work performed until the attorney-client relationship is terminated.

The ease of finding a good attorney can depend upon the nature of a case and the plaintiff's location. When it comes to common types of cases, such as personal injury or breach of contract, it usually isn't difficult to come up with a sufficient number of law firms to choose from. Many attorneys practice in these areas. If the matter involves workers' compensation law, defamation, or copyright infringement, the pickings can be slimmer because fewer attorneys practice in these areas. If you live in a metropolitan region where thousands of attorneys are concentrated, that may be a moot point. But in a rural area where the distribution of attorneys is thinner, it could affect your pickings.

Just as attorneys exhibit positive attributes that can be appealing, there are also red flags that could serve to steer you away from an attorney. After all, people can be in an emotional state of mind when they select an attorney. This can apply in commercial lawsuits, will contests, divorce proceedings, and other types of cases. If an attorney seems overly eager to hijack your emotions, that isn't a good sign. A plaintiff could be enticed into waging nuclear war in court, which might not always the best course of action for achieving an economical and reasonable resolution of a matter.

If an attorney becomes hostile at having legal fees questioned, that isn't a good sign either. It may be that he is experienced and good at what he does. However, that doesn't mean you're not entitled to question why a legal matter has to cost what it does. There may be less expensive routes to handling some of your issues that might not fit well with the attorney's agenda. If an attorney tells you, "This is how it's gonna be done," without having much patience for your own opinions, that could be a red flag. Attorneys aren't geniuses. They're professionals with a license to practice law.

An attorney isn't necessarily more intelligent than you. Presumably, he is more qualified than you to handle a legal matter. But since you're at a disadvantage here, the smart thing to do is to hold off on retaining an attorney you don't feel 100% comfortable with. It can be an indication that you need to conduct some research on your own, or get an opinion from another attorney. The first attorney could be correct in telling you, "This is how it's gonna be done." But that doesn't mean you're not entitled to figure out for yourself why that's so.

A big peeve of doctors is being asked for advice about medical problems at cocktail parties or other social occasions. "Oh, you're a doctor! Can I ask you this? I've been using Lipitor to lower my cholesterol for two months now. What do you think of the drug?" What does the doctor think? She thinks you should spend $30 of your co-pay to consult with a doctor who knows something about cholesterol management, that's what she thinks! The sentiments could be similar when someone tries to get inexpensive legal guidance in the same manner. What if that doctor is an orthopedic surgeon who handles sports injuries? She may know less about Lipitor than a retired chemist who does a lot of research about Lipitor on the internet.

This shows that it's worth the investment of time and money to get quality advice. One of the most dangerous mistakes a plaintiff can make is to act upon poor quality advice at the start. Every plaintiff is vulnerable to this. What's the first thing most people do when they contemplate bringing a legal action? They discuss it with their family at the dinner table. From this point on, wheels start spinning and the matter becomes a focal issue for the family.

Long after the dinner table has been cleared and dishes put away, family members put out their antennas to get advice for their loved one. They discuss the matter with friends. They discuss the matter at work. And what happens? Everyone provides input into the situation... some of it good and some of it bad. If the incoming information is bad, it can cause more harm than no advice at all. It's a good idea to speak with more than one person about your potential legal action. But it's also important to integrate all the information you receive in an intelligent manner.

What is the lesson of this chapter? A successful plaintiff carefully considers whether an attorney is necessary. If an attorney is necessary, a successful plaintiff diligently uses available resources to find an attorney who is competent and compatible to work with.

Tamara Kismet

The Successful Plaintiff Possesses Persistence and Determination

"Energy and persistence conquer all things."

Benjamin Franklin

Lawsuits involving large stakes can become battles of attrition. The more powerful side tries to wear down the weaker side. Just as a larger army can pour more troops into an infantry battle, a powerful adversary can pour more resources into a legal battle.

The plan is to exhaust and frustrate the weaker side until they ultimately give up the lawsuit, or settle on terms sought by the more powerful side. That's why the successful plaintiff must be persistent and determined. In business lawsuits, the more powerful side is usually a large corporation and the weaker side is usually an individual or small business owner.

In accident lawsuits, the more powerful side is usually an insurance company and the weaker side is usually an injury victim. A pedestrian struck by a speeding car wants to be compensated for the different ways in which she sustained damages. A construction company dismissed from a lucrative government contract after a vendor fails to deliver structural steel wants to be compensated for all the different ways in which it sustained damages.

Summary of Different Types of Damages in Lawsuits In a civil lawsuit, the underlying objective is generally money. The idea is that money will compensate the victim for damages sustained at the hands of a wrongdoer.

Economic Damages are given monetary values. They include bills for hospitals, ambulances, radiology services, prescription drugs, and other medical expenses. They include lost wages and property damage.

Non-economic Damages This is a funny choice of words. Non-economic damages are often the largest part of a lawsuit. They include pain and suffering, mental anguish, loss of affection, and loss of consortium.

Compensatory Damages are intended to restore a victim to a position she would have been in had she not been wronged in a transaction or business relationship.

Punitive Damages are used when a court wants to punish a wrongdoer for conduct that was deceitful or malicious. Punitive damages generally arise in transactional matters such as contracts.

A successful plaintiff sits down and figures out the dollar amount of damages she seeks in a lawsuit.

The injured pedestrian mentioned earlier would like to be able to walk again. She'd like to undergo physical therapy. She'd like enough money to make up for her pain and suffering. She'd like to be paid for the time she missed from work. Although the things she wants are reasonable, there will be a tug of war between what she feels she deserves and what the insurance company will offer her.

This classic tug of war can explain why seriously injured people sometimes settle their claims at unfairly low figures. It's often a one-sided battle. Between a multibillion dollar insurance company and an individual plaintiff, the plaintiff is at a disadvantage. People might think the opposite is true because our society traditionally pities the victim. When an accident victim is brought into court in a wheelchair, there won't be a dry eye in the jury. Jurors will make the insurance carrier write a ten million dollar check after viewing a tear-jerking "day in the life" film showing the plaintiff confined to bed most of the day.

That could hold true, but not every plaintiff is brought into court in a wheelchair. Not every plaintiff evokes a jury's sympathy. Not every plaintiff can stick it out for two years until a case comes up on the trial calendar. And not every juror is compassionate, especially in an economy where people are losing their jobs left and right. A juror who was recently laid off because his company moved its manufacturing to a third world country isn't likely to have lots of sympathy for a thirty year old male who says he's unable to work because of back pain. That's why insurance companies often wait and see who's on a jury before making meaningful offers to a plaintiff.

In the Joseph Heller novel *Catch-22*, American air crews wanted to get out of flying dangerous bombing missions during World War II. One way to do this was to be declared crazy. However, the Army Air Force used the argument that anyone who tried to avoid dangerous combat missions by claiming to be crazy couldn't really be crazy. A person would have to be quite sane to try to get out of combat duty. Therefore, it was impossible to be excused from the missions. The term "Catch-22" came to symbolize a situation where it was impossible to prevail against the system.

The legal system holds a certain Catch-22 for injury plaintiffs. When people are seriously injured at work, they are usually disabled. Disabled means they cannot return to work. As a result, they need to be supported by lost wage benefits during this period. For injuries arising in the course of employment, a state workers' compensation claim is filed. Federal employees file for federal workers' compensation benefits.

It seems like a good safety net. A plaintiff has money coming in so he won't be out on the street. But that's not the way it always works. These systems can be difficult to work with. The injured plaintiff can find himself in an adversarial contest, where a physician for the federal or state government might conclude that he can return to work. That physician is generally regarded as an independent physician, but he might feel pressure to clear people to return to work because doing otherwise could spell the end of his fruitful relationship with the government.

This means that injury victims who are disabled can find themselves forced to return to work through this mechanism of financial coercion. It plays well for the government and the insurance industry in two ways. It also creates a Catch-22 for plaintiffs. First off, the government and insurance industry save money by denying or delaying lost wages claims. Second, if a plaintiff later brings an action in court, he's told that his injuries couldn't be that severe if he was able to return to work in two short weeks. Plaintiffs who lack the means to stay out of work until their condition improves become victims in this Catch-22 that adds insult to injury.

This is somewhat similar to what happens in many car accidents. Many states operate under no-fault auto insurance systems, which means medical benefits are covered by your own carrier, whether you're at fault or not. Here's the funny part. After you start receiving medical treatment, such as physical therapy or chiropractic care, your insurance carrier generally schedules an exam for its physician to examine you. This is called an independent medical examination, but that physician is hired by the insurance company. Not surprisingly, many such physicians recommend termination of further benefits within a fairly conservative time period. If that happens, you can find yourself cut off from medical care.

But it gets better. To sustain a legal action for a motor vehicle accident, a plaintiff must often demonstrate that a serious physical injury took place. But when an insurance carrier moves quickly to cut off medical benefits, it can end access to the doctor whose treatment would serve to validate a serious injury. This can result in a case being dismissed from court. No case. No successful plaintiff. But *successful insurance carrier!*

Successful plaintiffs realize that if you're dealing with an insurance company in a lawsuit, be it your own or the adversary's, that insurance company looks out for number one. And number one is not you. In a way, they can't be blamed for this. Like all large corporations, insurance companies have an obligation to maximize profits for shareholders. And they do that very well. They also have strong pressure to keep customer premiums low in an industry which has become fiercely competitive.

This chapter begins with Benjamin Franklin's quote, "Energy and persistence conquer all things." Lawsuits back then were innocent affairs by today's standards. But the proverb holds true for modern day plaintiffs because a lawsuit can turn into a marathon. This is because of something known as *discovery*. Discovery is the process where parties in a lawsuit exchange information. It sounds like a good idea. You put your information on the table. I'll put my information on the table. Let's look at the pieces of this puzzle to see if we can come up with a fair and reasonable solution to our dispute. Ah, but if only it was that simple! That's not the way it works. Discovery is a process that can take years to complete in large lawsuits.

One reason for this is that discovery is more than just the simple process of exchanging information. It's a tool that powerful legal defendants abuse, by bullying and weakening their adversaries. In a lawsuit where the stakes are high, a plaintiff can face an adversary who demands volumes and volumes of information.

Discovery and the Deposition Trap Discovery is the process by which parties in a lawsuit exchange information. One of the tools used to do this is the *deposition*, sometimes called an *examination before trial*. In a deposition, a plaintiff answers questions under oath. Depositions are generally boring affairs that can tax a person's powers to stay awake. Here are some examples of information requested in a deposition:

- Please state your name for the record.

- Are you a resident of Ohio?

- On October 10, 2010, did you enter into a contract with the Ace Zeppelin Company?

You get the picture... it's dull. It's the legal equivalent of root canal. But the process holds a trap for the unwary. The plaintiff answers the adversary's questions thoroughly and courteously. The deposition transcript suggests a credible plaintiff. But ten months later, the adversary asks the plaintiff the same questions again. This time, it's in court before a jury. It's possible the plaintiff won't give identical answers to those same questions. Under the rules of evidence, this could qualify as a *prior inconsistent statement*, opening the door to discredit the credibility of the plaintiff.

A smart plaintiff won't let this trap spring on her. She'll review the transcript of the original deposition before answering any questions in this carefully orchestrated trap.

Discovery then becomes a sinister process where a plaintiff who obediently complies with requests to provide information finds himself hit with demands to provide even more information. It's the classic situation of,

"Well, your answer to that question just raises more questions." If you believe that, I've got a bridge I'd like to sell you!

Powerful legal adversaries like to turn the discovery process into what is known in the legal field as a "fishing trip." It's akin to throwing out a net and seeing what interesting things can be dragged up from the sea. Dragging things up in this net leads to opportunities for punching holes in a plaintiff's case. This isn't an accidental or incidental by-product of the discovery process. It's a premeditated strategy used by powerful adversaries to keep a smaller plaintiff at bay.

For the plaintiff facing a large adversary, the discovery process can be time-consuming and depleting. And that's because it's meant to be. For the large adversary, it's usually a joke, since it can crank out demands for discovery the way spam artists can crank out e-mails that clog up our home computers. When the stakes are high, the discovery process can become highly contentious because the more powerful side is in a win-win situation. A cooperating plaintiff could ultimately hang himself by putting everything on the table, while a hostile plaintiff can be declared uncooperative.

Successful plaintiffs never lose sight of the fact that a lawsuit or other type of legal action is a marathon and not a sprint. The system is designed to break the spirit and determination of the little guy. When a people file for federal disability, state disability, or workers' compensation benefits, they aren't necessarily approved for benefits in the first round of paperwork. Instead, the plaintiff often finds his disability claim denied for any number of reasons.

The claims examiner may declare that the underlying physical condition was pre-existing. The claims examiner may say the injury was not work-related. The claims examiner may declare that the injury is a recurrence of an earlier injury. It can go around in circles for months. The result is that the plaintiff finds his benefits denied. That's essentially the idea, because this type of aggressive resistance against plaintiffs can eliminate a good portion of claims right from the start.

It isn't until a plaintiff appeals the decision of the claims examiner that the tables may turn. In all fairness to the system, I have to point out that claims examiners are inundated by claims. And some of those claims are not always valid. Therefore, these systems often respond with a knee-jerk reaction to deny a large portion of benefit claims.

This succeeds in forcing many plaintiffs back to work. Even when a plaintiff is severely injured, the possibility of losing his house serves as a strong incentive to return to work. And that's generally the idea with these systems. There's a hard-nosed attitude that permeates throughout many government disability and work injury safety nets, with the collective goal of forcing plaintiffs back to work.

Although many successful plaintiffs succeed in appealing denials from insurance carriers or government entities, many lack the motivational or financial wherewithal to do this. That's why the system is akin to a marathon. It requires endurance and financial reserves to withstand months of stalemate, where checks are not coming in. The plaintiff with the fortitude to weather out the storm may find himself winning an appeal and getting months of back pay in one lump sum. But for many, that marathon is too grueling to endure.

What is the lesson of this chapter? A successful plaintiff realizes that lawsuits are often marathons, rather than sprints. A successful plaintiff prepares herself to encounter adversity and resistance in a lawsuit, and to not be demoralized by it.

The Successful Plaintiff Is Not Held Back by Fear

"Never let the fear of striking out get in your way."

Babe Ruth

Fear is an interesting emotion. Without it, we would have remarkably short life spans. Fear is the mechanism that keeps us from swimming a hundred yards offshore at a beach known to be frequented by great white sharks. Fear is the emotion that keeps us from bungee jumping off the Golden Gate Bridge. In these situations, fear has a useful purpose of self-preservation.

But look at the lives of successful people and you'll see they share a trait of not being held back by fear. It's not that these people didn't experience fear. They simply weren't *held back* by it. They weren't fools. They weren't reckless. But they weren't unnecessarily afraid of the consequences of their actions. Granted, some of them had money to absorb the consequences of bad decisions. Some had back-up careers. But in general, they took action fearlessly and prospered as a result. Life rewards those who take action.

And so it is with the successful plaintiff. The successful plaintiff is not held back by fear. When you initiate a lawsuit or a claim, there will always be things that create apprehension and fear. If it's a sexual harassment lawsuit, the plaintiff may fear the humiliation of having embarrassing intimate things revealed to the public. If it's a small business lawsuit, the plaintiff may fear a costly and depleting battle. If it's a lawsuit involving a workplace injury, a plaintiff may fear losing a job.

"You're going to sue us? Hah! Good luck working in this industry after a stunt like that!" Life can be a game of intimidation. The successful plaintiff does not buckle under intimidation. What are some of the dreadful things that an otherwise successful plaintiff might fear when contemplating a lawsuit? There are a myriad of things that can make a prospective plaintiff lose sleep.

What if the lawsuit leads to condemnation in the workplace? This is a possibility. For many people, their relationships in a workplace define their lives. To risk losing those things in an unsuccessful discrimination lawsuit or workers' compensation claim could create genuine concerns. But the successful plaintiff thinks past these concerns. If he feels his case has merit, the alternative of not taking action could be more troubling. If he was injured in the workplace and does nothing, he could be fired for any number of reasons down the road. At that point, he would have lost his opportunity to deal with the three herniated discs he'll be carrying around for the rest of his life.

What if the lawsuit leads to condemnation in the community? If the lawsuit is for injuries, a proud person might feel humiliated in declaring himself incapacitated. He might fear the judgment of friends who ask why he's always home. Neighbors could suggest he's feigning injury just to collect money. This happens with enough regularity in our society to bring frowns from the hard-working masses. Workers are experiencing unprecedented levels of stress on their jobs today, leaving them little compassion for the sight of a plaintiff shuffling around his kitchen in the middle of the day. But look at it this way. Would those neighbors be willing to pay this person's medical bills? Would they be willing to pay his lost wages?

What if the lawsuit leads to counterclaims? That's a possibility. We no longer live in a time when companies keel over and sprinkle money on plaintiffs who initiate legal actions. Just as people can learn the art of being *successful plaintiffs*, companies are accomplished in the art of being *successful defendants*. A simple lawsuit can turn into a grudge match, where the defendant turns around and sues the plaintiff for any number of things, some of which could have merit, and some of which have no other purpose than to discourage the lawsuit. Such aggressive responses are intended to make a plaintiff think twice about going forward with a lawsuit.

What if the lawsuit is laughed out of court? A plaintiff could be apprehensive about the fallout of an unsuccessful lawsuit that results in humiliation and defeat, instead of victory. The successful plaintiff doesn't concern himself with such fear. There's always a possibility of losing ANY lawsuit. But there's generally a higher probability of winning, even if victory is partial instead of total. Of course, this assumes that the lawsuit was a legitimate one with merit.

Times Have Changed During the Cold War Era, sexual values were very different than they are today. Romantic relationships were more restrictive, so far as premarital sex and cohabitation. However, even while society seemingly embraced wholesome values during the blissful decades following World War II, there was a paradoxical and disturbing manner in which rape cases were handled.

Defense attorneys would play a standard defense. They would bring forth male witnesses to testify that they knew the rape victim. They would give accounts of sexual activities with her. This circus was performed with one objective in mind, which was to make the rape victim appear promiscuous and indiscrete with men.

This practice was one of the sad travesties of justice during those years. For obvious reasons, this isn't the way rape trials are conducted today. Values have changed. Today, such defense attorneys and their entourages of clown witnesses would be laughed out of court at best... and face disciplinary charges at worst.

The point here is not to be burdened by fear of humiliation if you've been genuinely wronged. The other side probably has more to worry about than you do.

What if my neighbors find out I applied for Social Security Disability? My kids will be humiliated at school. At the supermarket, people will look at me as if I'm using food stamps. That's nonsense. Your neighbors don't receive announcements of Social Security Disability applicants in their local coupon flyers. It isn't a disgrace to be on disability if your reasons are legitimate. It could be more of a betrayal to your family if you're entitled to such benefits and don't apply for them, chipping away instead at savings and assets that should be preserved for retirement and children's educations.

What if my financial life is ruined by filing for bankruptcy? We've all heard the warnings to avoid bankruptcy. Filing for bankruptcy will make you ineligible to buy a house. You'll never be able to get a credit card again. Well, filing for bankruptcy is obviously not the best thing for one's credit score. But the process is used every day by multimillion dollar corporations to restructure their debts and financial liabilities. If someone has been overwhelmed by debt and is in danger of losing a house and other assets, bankruptcy might be the only solution. If a person is in serious enough financial straits to contemplate bankruptcy, it's likely their credit has already been damaged by chronic late payments.

What if a lawsuit results in intrusive personal investigations? This can be a concern for any plaintiff. What if the discovery process gets out of hand and the plaintiff is placed on the stand to answer questions about tax returns, mental illness, extramarital affairs, or public assistance? Everyone has skeletons in their closets. But that doesn't mean such things would be admissible in court. Your legal adversary is permitted to explore information which is relevant to a lawsuit. It might be the dream of an aggressive defense attorney to turn a sexual harassment lawsuit into an embarrassing carnival sideshow to humiliate a plaintiff. But that sort of thing happens on television shows more than it does in real life. Judges exercise discretion over the nature of information used in a trial. There's also the possibility that a matter could be settled before trial.

What if a lawsuit leads to problems with immigration status? This can be a concern for some plaintiffs. But the reality is that immigration status is generally not an issue in most lawsuits. Of all the causes of action discussed in this book, none require that a plaintiff be a U.S. citizen, or hold a green card. If someone is injured or damaged at the hands of a wrongdoer, her rights to recovery are independent of immigration status. Aggressive defendants may raise immigration status in lawsuits, but these attacks can generally be deflected.

What if sanctions are brought for a frivolous lawsuit? A person who uses a lawsuit to harass or bully an adversary should have genuine concerns about being accused of abusing the legal process. But that really isn't a concern for a legitimate plaintiff. By now, we know that *successful plaintiffs* do not initiate legal actions for the *wrong reasons*. They initiate them for legitimate causes of action that have merit.

What if the other side sues me for legal fees? That can happen, but it depends on the nature of the lawsuit and the laws in a given state. Unsuccessful plaintiffs have been sued for legal fees. It's best to check the laws in your particular state.

What if a lawsuit leads to criminal investigation that can send a plaintiff to jail? That's an issue that deep pocket defendants sometimes raise. If a plaintiff made false statements, that can constitute fraud. And fraud can be treated as a crime. Fraud could arise if a plaintiff made false statements in an effort to hide assets in a bankruptcy action. Fraud could arise if a plaintiff claimed injuries she didn't sustain. Fraud could arise if a company falsified financial records to hide the misconduct of corporate officers. If a plaintiff commits fraud, that could end the lawsuit and result in criminal charges. But successful plaintiffs do not commit fraud.

What Is Tort Reform? Tort reform is a movement aimed at reigning in the U.S. legal system to make it less lucrative for plaintiffs. It's a broad movement strongly supported by the insurance industry. Although the movement is focused on the tort industry, some of its goals can impact other areas of law as well. Tort reform calls for sanctions and penalties for frivolous lawsuits.

Tort reformists argue that injured plaintiffs need to be held accountable for their actions. In other words, just because you were injured, it doesn't necessarily mean someone else is responsible. Tort reform calls for money caps on pain and suffering awards in injury and medical malpractice lawsuits. This aspect of tort reform is the result of lawsuits where juries have awarded mind-boggling sums of money to some plaintiffs.

Aside from these fears, there is another type of fear that concerns plaintiffs. It's the fear of losing control over a matter when a lawsuit is filed. This is a well-founded fear, because the act of suing someone changes the playing field. The following scenario should illustrate the point.

A freelance writer has developed material for an advertising agency. The agency refuses to pay him, arguing that the work did not meet their editorial guidelines. The writer brings a lawsuit in civil court.

What is Fraud? In layman's terms, fraud is lying and deceit. In legal terms, fraud arises when someone:

- makes a false statement about something,

- makes the statement intentionally,

- knows the statement is false,

- knows the other side will rely on the statement to act or refrain from acting in a certain manner, and

- the other side sustains damages as a result of relying on the false statement.

Before the writer commenced the lawsuit, he and the advertising agency enjoyed a reasonable degree of control over the way they handled their disputes. They enjoyed control in terms of being able to speak with each other freely on the telephone. They enjoyed control in terms of being able to freely exchange e-mails. They enjoyed control in terms of being able to meet in a coffee shop to hash out their disagreements. But commencing a lawsuit changed all that.

Why does the element of control diminish when a lawsuit is commenced? Let's look at the sequence of events in a lawsuit and how it serves to constrict a plaintiff's conduct. A lawsuit begins when the plaintiff serves the defendant with a *summons and complaint*. These formal legal papers identify the parties in a lawsuit, the facts, the legal causes of action, and the amount of money demanded from the defendant.

Some plaintiffs believe that serving a summons and complaint will bring about a quick resolution of a dispute. This line of reasoning has its merits. A defendant who receives a summons and complaint realizes the other side means business. The gloves are off! The defendant wonders if it makes more sense to give the plaintiff what he wants so that this whole mess goes away. But not all defendants keel over and die when they're sued. In some types of actions, such as medical collections, a summons and complaint can spur a debtor into paying a hospital bill.

But in cases involving greater stakes, a defendant may just decide to dig her heels in and fight. So much for the notion that everybody trembles when served with legal papers. Being sued has become more commonplace today. It's never pleasant, but being sued doesn't necessary bring paralyzing fear to all defendants. Instead, a tough defendant will respond to the original summons and complaint. That response will be in the form of legal papers called an *answer*.

In her answer, the defendant will address each element of the plaintiff's summons and complaint. To the disappointment of many plaintiffs, defendants often categorically deny everything a plaintiff alleges. In other words, "I did not do the things you say I did."

Defendants also like to assert that they lack knowledge of the plaintiff's allegations. In other words, "I have no idea what you're talking about." This makes it apparent to the plaintiff that there won't be any quick settlement here. This endeavor is going to be stressful. This unpleasant affair will require extracting information from a defendant the hard way.

And that's why a plaintiff can be afraid of losing control. A plaintiff who once enjoyed the freedom of picking up the phone and haggling over a legal dispute is now bound by formal legal procedure. And the sequence of events only thickens. With the *answer*, a defendant can include a *demand for a bill of particulars*. This requires the plaintiff to address the factual and legal basis of allegations made in the *summons and complaint*. The plaintiff may not have realized that things would become this sticky.

The process of exchanging all these formal legal papers is part of the pre-trial stage of a lawsuit. This stage also includes demands for discovery. *Discovery* is a nine-letter word, but at the same time, a four-letter word for many plaintiffs. Discovery means money, expense, intrusion, uncertainty, and getting stuck in muck. That's because discovery can go on for what can seem to be an eternity.

Discovery, which is discussed in the previous chapter, is the process where the plaintiff and defendant exchange information. Discovery can involve summoning the plaintiff to appear for a deposition. It can involve serving the plaintiff with interrogatories, which are written questions. It can involve summoning the plaintiff to present herself for a physical examination if the lawsuit involves personal injury.

Finding Evidence on eBay? At one time or another, most of us have purchased something on eBay, the online auction site. There's something magical about place where you can bid on Barbie dolls and old Lionel trains. But we never think of eBay as a place where trial lawyers search for evidence. People sometimes sell old training manuals or industrial products online, either for their historic value or to clean out their attics. Most shoppers have no interest in such items.

But for attorneys who know what they're looking for, those things could be valuable. Let's say an attorney represents a shipyard laborer who comes down with a respiratory illness twenty years after retirement. The laborer says he wasn't told to use protective equipment while stripping insulation from old steam turbines and piping. The shipyard argues it wasn't aware of health hazards associated with stripping the insulation. But training manuals from the period might show the industry was well aware of certain health hazards.

eBay isn't your typical legal research tool. But some attorneys look for these kinds of things because they could serve as compelling evidence for a jury.

Discovery can also include demands for physical evidence, such as damaged property. It can include demands for official documents, such as incident reports, contracts, affidavits, or inspection surveys. It's apparent that discovery can become a lengthy and costly endeavor that the plaintiff never really wanted.

So while I say that successful plaintiffs are not held back by fear, I have to temper that with the caveat that initiating a lawsuit can open the door to uncertainty. A plaintiff's worst fears of losing control over the course of a dispute can be compounded in another way. If the defendant hires an attorney, that attorney might not necessarily want the matter to be resolved quickly and inexpensively. That attorney could be paid by the hour, which means he stands to make more money if the lawsuit drags on for a long time.

After the discovery process is completed, a lawsuit is ready for the trial stage. Many lawsuits never reach this stage. That's because the plaintiff and defendant usually don't want to go through a trial unless there's something very big at stake. But if things do make it this far, a plaintiff could be called to patiently answer the same stupid deposition questions in a courtroom setting. Since the courtroom setting is meant to verify everyone's truthfulness, it's a rigidly choreographed stage where players must follow strict rules.

When a plaintiff answers questions in court, the stage directions are rigid and narrow. It's basically a setting of, "I'm asking the questions. Answer them in exactly the same manner I'm asking them." This means the questions might be framed to have only "yes" or "no" answers. The plaintiff can't say, "Well, yes, that's true. But there's more to it. You see, your guy ripped me off two years ago when he failed to make payments on lumber and concrete I delivered to his construction site. He wrote bad checks... " In this setting, a plaintiff is no longer a regular person having a conversation with the defendant. The plaintiff is now an actor on stage in a hostile interrogation designed to make him look bad.

For the uninitiated, it can be a bizarre setting. Imagine you're having breakfast on Saturday morning and your spouse asks, "Honey, did you have the car inspected yesterday?" You reply, "I was going to, but you wanted me to pick the kids up from your mom's house." Your spouse replies, "Yes, or no… did you, or did you not, have the car inspected?" You reply, "How could I have the car inspected when I'm stopping at your mom's house?" Your spouse turns around to your mother and says, "The witness is being unresponsive." You raise your voice to protest this insanity, adding, "You're the one who asked me to stop at your mom's house!" Your spouse turns to your mother and says, "I ask the court to declare Mr. Smith a hostile witness."

It's a crazy scenario that seems more like a comedy skit than reality, but the point is that going to court means relinquishing freedom in a legal matter. Before things wound up in court, you experienced total freedom in the manner and form of communications with the other side… by phone, e-mail, or fax. It's certainly more difficult to accomplish things within the formal confines of depositions and cross-examinations. But look at it this way. If the dispute deteriorated to the point where court became the only viable option, you probably didn't have tremendous control over the matter anyway.

What is the lesson of this chapter? A successful plaintiff does not allow himself to be held back by fear in a legal matter. He may have reservations. He may have apprehensions about the outcome of things. But he doesn't become paralyzed by fear.

The Successful Plaintiff Understands the Power of Perception

"Men are disturbed not by things, but by the view which they take of them."

Epictetus

What is a magician? I don't mean to insult anyone's intelligence with that question. Everyone knows a magician is someone who performs magic, which is a form of illusion. A magician uses sleight of hand to pull a rabbit out of a hat, or pluck an Ace of Clubs out of a seemingly random deck of cards. Where is this line of reasoning going? Am I suggesting that plaintiffs practice the art of illusion to deceive members of a jury? Of course not!

But I will say that a successful plaintiff puts on a show for a jury... a show that can arguably be called an act of illusion. It would be wrong to call this show a fraud. But it would be correct to call this show a successful orchestration of perception. Instead of magic, the act of the plaintiff involves a performance of words. And just as a magician doesn't share with an audience the workings of a secret trap door, the successful plaintiff doesn't share with a court the information she leaves behind the curtain. The plaintiff's performance hinges on highlighting facts that support her position, and leaving out those that get in the way.

The ethical balance here lies in the fact that there is a sideshow, which is the complementary performance by the defendant. The defendant's "sideshow" tries to make the plaintiff's performance look like a sham. And that's the way our civil justice system works. Things work this way in the criminal justice system as well.

A prosecutor doesn't ask a jury look at a murder case the same way a law professor asks her students to analyze it in a criminal law class. If things worked like that, jurors would consider facts that a prosecutor wouldn't want them to consider. Instead, a prosecutor asks a jury to look at a murder case from the position he argues from... a position aimed at putting the defendant in jail.

When you think about it, comparing a legal proceeding to a magic show isn't so far-fetched. In a magic show, success of the performance hinges on an audience's perception of what it sees. And so it is in the courtroom. Many things in life hinge upon a viewer's perception.

Let's illustrate the concept with an unhappy couple. A husband and wife are going through a divorce. They're in their late thirties, with three small children. Here's a description of the husband by the wife's sister...

"He's been married to my sister for about fifteen years now. In all those years, I've never seen him lift a finger to clear the table after a meal. He works an easy job with the state. When he gets home, he greets the kids as if my sister isn't even in the room. I remember times when my sister would be changing diapers on their youngest while preparing snacks for the older two, with the dishwasher going, and dinner cooking on the stove. He'd be watching TV in the other room, pretending not to notice. He's come on to me twice at our family holiday parties. He abuses my sister with his stupid comments about her weight and her homemaker lifestyle. He makes fun of her when she expresses a desire to go back to school. He deliberately humiliates my sister by complimenting her female friends about their athletic figures... right in front of her at little league games. Meanwhile, my poor sister doesn't have 30 free minutes in her hectic day to get on a treadmill. I think the best was when he blew the family off for a week to volunteer for a local fundraising event, which was basically a week of pizza and socializing with female co-workers after work. He's a miserable, passive-aggressive, cruel piece of garbage."

Obviously, the wife's sister doesn't think very highly of her brother-in-law.

Now here's a description of the same guy by his own sister...

> "He's an awesome dad. I remember one year, he was up until three in the morning putting together a bicycle for their oldest daughter's birthday. He works his tail off five days a week so he can give his family a good quality of life. He doesn't buy a thing for himself. The kids always come first. His only refuge is the TV set, where he can enjoy a little peace from that woman's incessant whining about how hard she has it. Except for the smallest child, the kids are pretty much self-sufficient. I don't even know what she does all day. At work, my brother volunteered for the annual town fundraiser, where he painted banners, put up signs, and built booths to raise money for the local high school. He's amazing... with three kids at home, he still finds time to give to the community. And he coaches little league softball on Saturdays. He's a dream dad. But nothing he does is enough for that woman. Every time I call the house, I hear the TV set going in the background. I wouldn't be surprised if my brother collapsed one day from all the misery that ungrateful woman gives him. If that ever happened, she'd have the rest of her life to think about how she took my brother for granted."

Wow! Is that the same husband they're talking about? It is. And it goes to show how the presentation of information to a jury can evoke very different feelings... from sympathy, to admiration, to animosity. It all depends on how something is *perceived*. And that delivery of perception hinges on the performance of the plaintiff in this "magic show." Depending on which witness is more convincing on the witness stand, jurors could walk away with vastly different sentiments about the husband.

This concept of perception applies to so many legal issues. We're all aware of the phenomenon known as identity theft. It costs Americans billions of dollars every year. The consequences include damage to credit scores and feelings of personal violation. The common perception of identity theft is that a criminal steals vital personal information and uses it to apply for credit cards. A common technique is for thieves to "phish" for personal information with bogus e-mails that say things like, "Your bank account has been frozen." The victim is asked to log into a system. If he isn't wise to the scam, he winds up divulging personal information.

But let's think about something for a moment. The criminal steals your information and poses as you to a financial institution. When the criminal racks up all sorts of debt, the financial institution comes after you. What is the perception here? It's that YOU were responsible for your personal information falling into the hands of criminals. But wait a second. Those criminals approached the financial institution and they posed as you.

Why isn't the financial institution responsible here? They were duped just like the individual victim. If anything, a multibillion dollar bank has better resources to prevent this sort of thing than an elderly widow. But that's not the way things are perceived in identity theft, is it? That's because society has been indoctrinated with the *perception* that the individual is responsible for the violation. It's all about *perception!*

Perception is all about how things are presented. Perception can trump common sense if it's controlled correctly. Remember all the energy crises we've had, both real and fabricated? You'd buy a cup of coffee for a buck, but some stores wouldn't give you plastic lid. The reason was that they wanted to do their part to reduce the consumption of hydrocarbons. Look how the art of perception makes a cost-cutting merchant appear like a thoughtful person who cares about the environment.

Perception doesn't only impact judges and juries. It impacts lawmakers. The issue of workplace internships may illustrate this. In some states, legislators are calling for laws to prevent the abuse of internships. We're all familiar with the institution of the internship as a means for students to get their foot in the door with good companies. It's supposed to be a win-win situation. The intern gets valuable experience and the company gets a bright kid for a few months.

However, internships are not what they used to be. There are many jobless college grads out there. They face difficult prospects for employment. Alert companies have picked up on this desperate state of affairs, offering unpaid internships as a preferable alternative to sitting at home and mailing out resumes. Lawmakers argue that this new generation of internships essentially amounts to having people work for free. Look at the element of perception here. The companies say interns gain valuable experience. Lawmakers say the companies are violating wage laws by having people work for free. Which is it? It all depends on the *perception* of the observer.

What is the lesson of this chapter? A successful plaintiff works hard to deliver the perception that her lawsuit is worthy. She does this by carefully controlling the facts she presents, emphasizing those that support her position.

Tamara Kismet

The Successful Plaintiff Practices the Golden Rule

"One should treat others as one would like others to treat oneself."

The Golden Rule

The golden rule is as old as time itself. It's a universal code of conduct that appears in Christianity, Judaism, Islam, and other religions. Its universal appeal may lie in its simplicity. It touches many aspects of our lives, from work to friendships. But what does it have to do with being a successful plaintiff? More than you may realize.

The relevance of the golden rule in legal settings may not be readily apparent, largely because the rule often applies to things a plaintiff does BEFORE a lawsuit materializes. And hopefully, people follow the golden rule to be better human beings, and not better plaintiffs. Nonetheless, the rule is an inescapable element of the legal process.

Living by the golden rule simply means being decent to people. If you're an employer, it means treating people fairly. It means paying them adequately. It means not exploiting them. It means not doing malicious things to them. By corollary, this may suggest that not following the golden rule makes one a better defendant. It does.

That's because it's easier to sue people who are hated than people who are liked. That isn't a quote from a renowned law professor. It's simply the way the world works. It's important to understand that lawsuits often hinge upon testimony from witnesses. In employment discrimination or sexual harassment actions, the victim's claims need to be supported by witnesses. Otherwise, it simply turns into a matter of "he said-she said."

We've all seen lawsuits where we thought to ourselves, "Why would people be so stupid as to say things like that in the workplace?" Well, the record showed that they did, and that's all that mattered. But a more critical question is not *why* some idiot said such stupid things. It's more about why people would *go out of their way to testify* against the person.

Odds are good that the person who committed the wrongful act was seriously disliked. Co-workers were just waiting for a chance to hurt this person. Their sense of civility could have been offended by a mean-spirited supervisor who went out of her way to reprimand her secretary for petty things. Their sense of decency could have been offended by a manager's sexually offensive and disturbing comments. People who are disliked, whether in the workplace or other settings, have been cause for some of the best testimony that plaintiffs could have ever wished for. Our legal system has rewarded many plaintiffs, and punished many defendants, often on nothing more than the mere words of others.

> **What is Evidence?** Evidence is information that's presented in court. That sounds simple enough, but the rules of evidence are complex. In general, evidence is admissible (allowable) if it is relevant to the issue at hand.
>
> The reason we have rules of evidence is to control the quality and quantity of information presented in court. Otherwise, jurors would be overwhelmed by more information than they could process.
>
> The task of filtering out extraneous evidence belongs to the judge. The control of evidence is a crucial element in what a jury will *perceive*, which you can appreciate from the previous chapter.

Does this mean that witnesses would exaggerate events... or worse, lie about events in court? Well, it wouldn't be the first time it happened. Surprising as it may seem, people lie. The fact that they're under oath only tends to discourage the less adept liars. Although we like to take comfort in the fact that witnesses testify about actual facts in a given matter, it isn't uncommon for people to allow their sentiments to get in the way.

Sentiments can be stronger than reality. Imagine a prison yard setting where an inmate says, "This prison sucks." All the inmates think the prison sucks. But the sentiments towards this particular inmate rallies other inmates to say, "What do you mean this prison sucks? Maybe you're the one with the problem!" Incongruously, the other inmates seem ready to defend the honor of their miserable prison against the hated inmate. And that kind of alignment of sentiments can produce surprising forms of testimony.

It only goes to show that everyone is human, and comes equipped with a full range of human weaknesses. Think of jurors. Jurors are supposed to make decisions based on the facts before them in a trial. The idea is a jury of one's peers. Do you think that jurors don't allow personal feelings to get in the way? Do you think jurors exercise so much control over their feelings that they conduct themselves like computers, solely analyzing facts and suppressing their personal biases?

> **The Hearsay Rule** This rule governs how statements made outside of court can be offered as evidence. The Federal Rules of Evidence define hearsay as a "statement, other than one made by the declarant while testifying at the trial or hearing, offered in evidence to prove the truth of the matter asserted."
>
> The basic reason for the rule is that unless the person who made a statement is physically in the courtroom, subject to questioning, courts will not accept the truthfulness of the statement's contents at face value.

They do not. Jurors are human beings. They are given to likes, dislikes, prejudices, and whims. They take dislikes to people's hairstyles. They take dislikes to people's accents. They take likes to people's fashion sense. Go figure... because no one can. Jurors can decide things any which way they like. Jurors aren't subjected to a polygraph test to determine if their votes were based on objective analysis, or personal likes and dislikes. In truth, our legal system is considerably more subjective than we would like to take comfort in believing.

The "He Said-She Said" Rule The hearsay rule is an important part of the rules of evidence. It's one of those things that every law school graduate knows verbatim the night before the bar exam. However, there's another rule, which I call the "he said-she said" rule. You won't find the rule in any legal dictionary. But it's a good way to describe the operation of the rules of evidence.

Legal disputes often turn into situations of "he said-she said." If two people collide at a traffic light and both insist the light was green for them, it's impossible to prove who is lying. Other things being equal, witnesses or jurors will tend to take sides with a person they like more than a person they dislike.

Adherence to the golden rule applies in all types of lawsuits, not just those involving employee discrimination, sexual harassment, or slander. In breach of contract lawsuits, it's easy to say that an issue is black or white, based upon the written terms of a contract. But once the ink dries, things become more complex.

In many situations, parties to a contract make changes in the terms, often verbally. For instance, let's say a textile supplier makes an agreement to deliver materials to the warehouse of a clothing manufacturer at 12:00 noon every Friday. Because of traffic delays, the two companies find it difficult to adhere to this schedule. Things become more informal and relaxed with the passage of time. The textile supplier starts to make deliveries in the middle of the week on any given day.

Let's say the clothing manufacturer doesn't appreciate the fact that deliveries are now randomly made, whenever convenient for the textile supplier. Under these circumstances, the clothing manufacturer could turn around and accuse the textile supplier of being in breach of their contract.

In confronting these accusations, employees from both companies could be called in to testify that key personnel on both sides verbally agreed it was okay to make deliveries whenever convenient, rather than the strict Friday schedule. The testimony of these employees could be influenced by their sentiments towards their respective employers. If their employers treated them well and followed the golden rule, the employees would be likely to say things to protect their employers.

What is the lesson of this chapter? A successful plaintiff follows the golden rule and exploits advantages that arise when her adversary violates the golden rule.

The Successful Plaintiff Understands the Art of Negotiation

"Negotiation in the classic diplomatic sense assumes parties more anxious to agree than to disagree."

Dean Acheson

Dean Acheson was Secretary of State for President Harry S Truman from 1949 to 1953. He shaped U.S. foreign policy during the Cold War and advised President John F. Kennedy during the Cuban Missile Crisis. His quote is in the context of diplomatic and foreign policy negotiations. However, it holds true for legal negotiations as well.

There may be times where both parties aren't necessarily anxious to agree. A plaintiff may want to drag the defendant through the mud in a full-blown trial, or vice versa. A defendant may rather pay $20,000 in legal fees than pay a $2,000 settlement award, simply because he feels the plaintiff is a dirtbag. Negotiation could be unlikely if the legal action seeks to prevent a shopping center from being built on a wildlife refuge. Plaintiffs may not want to negotiate anything short of a complete halt of construction.

But in many civil actions, there's an incentive for both sides to come to the negotiating table. This mutual incentive is the avoidance of a lawsuit that can drag on for years. Lawsuits are expensive affairs. Although both sides may "rattle sabers" and claim they're willing to fight to the bitter end, the possibility of a less costly resolution is usually appealing for both sides.

A major reason for the costly nature of lawsuits is the discovery process, which was discussed in earlier chapters. Discovery can eat up the budget of a small plaintiff. Discovery can take months, sometimes years, to complete. It can require testimony from expert witnesses, who don't come cheaply. If the matter involves personal injury, physicians could be called in to testify about the severity of a plaintiff's disability and prognosis for future recovery. When reputable physicians take time out from their surgery schedules to testify in court, they easily charge $750 an hour.

And the process doesn't end with one expert's testimony. It becomes a showdown of medical, scientific, engineering, or financial expertise that pits one side's budget against the other's. By the time the dust settles, expert testimony can run into tens of thousands of dollars. Most plaintiffs aren't comfortable advancing that kind of money.

Before a plaintiff comes to the negotiating table, he must have an idea of what he wants to accomplish. When a plaintiff serves the defendant with a summons and complaint, it generally includes a demand for a sum of money. Although many negligence lawsuits settle for less than $10,000, that doesn't stop attorneys from making demands for $3 million, $5 million, or $10 million at the outset... even in the most humble cases.

Negotiation Is Also an Important Aspect of the Criminal Justice System We see negotiation as an important part of personal injury, contract, and other civil lawsuits. But it's just as important in the criminal justice system.

Think of the plea bargain. A prosecutor may sit down with a criminal defendant and advise him that he's looking at a ten year prison sentence for armed robbery. The prosecutor may offer the defendant a chance to plead guilty to a lesser charge with a shorter jail sentence to avoid the risk of a criminal trial. It's not all one-sided. The prosecutor may have holes in his own case. Both sides see the plea bargain as an avoidance of risk.

Seasoned plaintiffs and defendants realize that such sums of money are but matters of fantasy. Yet there seems to be a tendency to ask for the moon and stars. Some attorneys feel that to ask for less might invite malpractice claims. Some attorneys simply have those dollar amounts fixed in their word processing templates. Whatever the case, there must be a realistic basis for demanding a sum of money in a lawsuit... be it pain and suffering, medical expenses, lost wages, or property damage. If the money demanded bears no realistic connection to the damages at hand, there will be an impasse.

An important aspect of negotiation is that the end result must be tenable for both sides. A plaintiff may tell himself, "I want to walk away from this case with $400,000." If the merits and damages of the case don't add up to that figure, *it ain't gonna happen!* About thirty or forty years ago, it was easier to negotiate settlements... settlements of all kinds. In those days, when lawsuits were initiated, the parties often came to the bargaining table. The economy was better and there was a less aggressive attitude towards plaintiffs. Maybe the fact that there were fewer plaintiffs back then also had something to do with it.

But times have changed. Companies and individuals today are sued with less hesitation. Plaintiffs routinely represent themselves in small claims court and civil court, meaning that the so-called "keys to the courthouse" are not some exclusive privilege placed high up on a shelf. The dockets of lower courts are bursting at the seams in many large cities. There are more laws today, meaning there are more ways in which businesses and individuals can run afoul of those laws. Companies can be sued under the Americans with Disabilities Act, employee right-to-know laws, smoking policies, and tons of other laws that can be complex in nature.

More laws, larger populations, more sophisticated and well-informed citizens, a deteriorating economy, and an overall decline in quality of life have all contributed to the proliferation of lawsuits. The result is that defendants today no longer keel over and die when they're sued. They rally up their defenses and fight back. Some defendants see plaintiffs as pillagers. Some defendants take a posture of *millions for defense but not one penny for tribute*. Some defendants see plaintiffs as the scourge of the earth. And then there are defendants who have a soft side for plaintiffs, but nonetheless, see them as a threat… *"I feel your pain, but you're not going to get a penny out of me for that pain!"*

A successful plaintiff knows that his demand for relief will often be rebuffed. A knee-jerk reaction of many defendants is to say there is no case… or that if there IS a case, the damages aren't what the plaintiff claims they are. That's pretty much a given, unless a defendant's position is so weak that the only thing left to do is write the plaintiff a check. But even in those situations, a diligent defendant still looks for reasons to pay less.

As mentioned earlier, a successful plaintiff realizes the defendant must walk away from the negotiation table with something. Otherwise, the defendant has no incentive to negotiate. That's why it's called negotiation. It isn't called piñata, the birthday party game where kids whack a stuffed object until it spills out toys and candy. A smart plaintiff doesn't wear two catcher's mitts while uttering, "gimme, gimme." She wears a catcher's mitt on one hand and uses the other hand to throw balls for the defendant to catch.

Let's say a plaintiff demands $75,000 to settle a commercial dispute. Let's say the defendant stands to lose $75,000 under the very worst circumstances… if all the stars and planets line up to deliver him the worst attorney his law firm can send to court on the day of trial, the worst judge, and the worst jury. Under these conditions, the defendant has no reason to settle for $75,000. Why fork over money a plaintiff would have to fight for, and possibly not win?

What Is a Class Action Lawsuit? A class action lawsuit lumps together a group of plaintiffs into a single lawsuit. Class action lawsuits are commonly used in asbestos exposure cases, tobacco cases, or dangerous automobile cases.

If a thousand people are suing the maker of a flu medicine for its failure to warn users about side effects, it's more economical for them to proceed with a single lawsuit rather than a thousand lawsuits. The cost of expert testimony is shared by many, instead of a few.

However, critics argue that class action lawsuits are used to abuse the system and to leverage settlements out of companies in an unfair manner.

Why do parties negotiate? They might both have strong incentives to avoid going to the courthouse, which can be similar to going to the racetrack. You don't know if you're going to come back with winnings, or if you're going to lose money. For those who see things from a gambler's point of view, a lawsuit is a game of chance. Some horses run fast and some run slow. Some judges are tough and some are soft. Some jurors are generous and some are hostile. It's all a gamble.

The outcome of a lawsuit is very much like gambling in some ways. And we know that gambling has a lot to do with mathematics and probability. If you don't agree, just ask card counters who are unwelcome at certain casinos because they won too many games of blackjack. Like casinos and racetracks, courthouses offer plaintiffs certain *odds* at winning. Insurance companies understand these odds. They weigh these odds in deciding whether to settle a case or defend a case.

Insurance companies will often base their decision to settle or defend a case by weighing a number of factors. These include the county where a case will be heard, the money limits on the insurance policy, the judge who will preside over the case, the demographic and political profile of jurors in the county, the rating of the plaintiff attorney, the amount of damages, the documentation of damages, and the strength of expert witnesses. If odds favor playing hardball, they'll do that. If odds favor loosening the purse strings to avoid a bigger loss at the hands of a "plaintiff-friendly" courtroom, they'll do that as well. Successful plaintiffs similarly weigh these same factors.

When presenting a money demand to the defendant, a successful plaintiff asks for more than she hopes to walk away with. One doesn't need to graduate from a prestigious business school to appreciate this concept. It's almost a matter of common sense. When kids swap toys in the schoolyard, they wheel and deal for a little more than what they hope to walk away with. This is basic human nature at its best... or worst, depending on your perspective.

The bargaining cushion in a plaintiff's demand needs to be appropriate for the matter at hand. While there is no hard fast rule of thumb, it's customary for plaintiffs to ask for 20% to 25% more than the figure at which they hope to settle a case. If a defendant rejects the demand, this leaves the door open for further negotiations. Successful plaintiffs always give themselves such a safety margin.

But there's a catch to this approach. Some plaintiffs feel that if it's a good idea to ask for 25% more than a target settlement, it could be even better to ask for 75% more. That way, you make out really well! But it doesn't work like that. Defendants and insurance companies aren't stupid. The peril of suggesting a disproportionately large demand is that it can backfire.

It can backfire because greed offends most people. The resulting animosity can damage prospects for continued negotiations. If the defendant had a decent settlement figure in mind at the outset of negotiations, she might reconsider it if a plaintiff's greed offended her sufficiently. It's natural to want *more*.

Everyone wants *more*. Have you ever watched a kid being served at an ice cream shop? Like a cat watching a mouse, the kid's eyes follow every move of the ice cream server's hand. How much ice cream is he scooping up? Is he giving me the good stuff in the middle, or the refrozen sludge along the edges? Every negotiating plaintiff was at one time or another, a kid at an ice cream shop. Those human qualities don't change. But the successful plaintiff knows how to prevent those qualities from damaging the course of negotiations.

In spite of a plaintiff's best efforts, there may be times when negotiation isn't possible. The art of negotiation hinges upon a desire by *both* sides to come to the table. An insurance company may pose an attractive offer to a plaintiff when its policyholder was intoxicated and caused a serious accident. A prosecutor could want to negotiate a plea bargain if he sees a charming defendant who would be well-liked by a jury. In such situations, it's a two-way street.

But it doesn't always work like that. A bad economy can dampen the chances for a two-way street in negotiations. This is often the case in labor law matters. A company may not be interested in negotiating for resolution of a labor dispute. It may tell union representatives, "This is the new contract. Take it or leave it." The company may have lined up manufacturing facilities overseas. It could be determined to break a union. In such situations, there may be no choice but to accept the terms or reject the terms.

What is the lesson of this chapter? A successful plaintiff negotiates with skill. She thoughtfully considers the dollar amount she seeks, and explores how that fits in with the expectations of the defendant.

The Successful Plaintiff Adapts to Factors that Cannot be Controlled

"We cannot direct the wind, but we can adjust the sails."

Bertha Calloway

A successful plaintiff studies a battle plan before making the first move in a legal action. Like a game of chess, there are time-tested opening moves and strategies. But a lawsuit doesn't always work like a game of chess.

You start with a good plan. But things take unexpected turns. More than a game of chess, a lawsuit can turn into a game of *Monopoly*, where the other side owns Boardwalk with a hotel on it, and you only own Short Line Railroad. It can be like a game of *Tetris*, where you need the next piece to be a nice straight rod, but instead, you get that crooked piece that doesn't fit anywhere. A lawsuit is a game that's part skill, part luck, and part adaptability to tough situations.

A good example of plaintiffs adapting to a tough situation took place with the tragic Staten Island Ferry accident in New York City. On October 15,

2003, the ferry *Andrew J. Barberi* crashed into a concrete and steel pier at St. George Terminal in Staten Island. She was estimated to be steaming at approximately 16 knots, which was her normal sea speed. Ten passengers were killed in the crash, with one more dying from injuries two months later. More than sixty passengers were injured. Investigations revealed the ferry pilot lost consciousness at the helm and that he had been on medication.

In the aftermath of the tragic disaster, the City of New York was hit with massive personal injury and wrongful death actions from passengers and their families. The City acted swiftly to protect itself. It filed a complaint in federal court to limit its liability to the post-accident value of the ferry. It did this by invoking the Limitation of Shipowners' Liability Act of 1851, hereafter referred to as the *limitation act.*

This *limitation act* is a tricky piece of ancient maritime law. It would have enabled the City of New York to reduce payments to accident victims and their families. That would have been good for the City, but bad for the plaintiffs. The arcane law arose at a time when square-rigged sailing ships crowded New York Harbor. In essence, it says a ship owner isn't responsible for losses beyond the value of the ship if an accident was caused by factors beyond his control. The purpose of the law was to encourage mercantile trade during the 1800s.

If the City of New York had been able to demonstrate that it didn't have control over the factors that caused the accident, it would have succeeded in invoking the law, thus limiting its liability. But the plaintiffs successfully argued that the causes of the accident WERE within the City's control. They used the findings of the National Transportation Safety Board, which concluded that the City failed to establish effective safety procedures for its fleet.

As a result, the City had to pay full fare to victims and their families. But consider the facts. The City of New York attempts to use a unique provision of maritime law which can be difficult to challenge. The plaintiffs challenge the use of the law and defeat the City's efforts to limit its liability. This was a complex case involving extensive fact-finding. And it demonstrates the power of plaintiffs who are able to adapt to formidable obstacles in a lawsuit.

The ability to be adaptive is useful in almost every legal setting. Plaintiffs often find themselves in tough spots against badly written and unfair laws. Being adaptive means arguing against a problematic law in creative ways. It doesn't mean jumping up and down and crying that the law is bad, *"because it hurts my position!"* That would be self-serving and a judge would have no patience for it.

An adaptive plaintiff argues that the problematic law wasn't intended for situations such as hers. Let's go back to the limitation law the City of New

York tried to use against accident victims in the Staten Island Ferry accident. If a passenger is injured on a cruise ship, the cruise line would use that same law. The adaptive plaintiff would make arguments about the *legislative intent* of limitation law.

By arguing about the *legislative intent* of the law, she tells the court, "Look, this law was written in the nineteenth century to help the shipping industry. Without the law, ship owners wouldn't have had an incentive to build the clipper ships that helped American commerce grow. But I was injured on a cruise ship in the year 2011, not the year 1860. I was injured because the cruise line let someone who didn't know to handle a jet ski loose on the water. This idiot crashed into my jet ski. My hip was fractured. I suffered a concussion. It took over a hundred stitches to put my face back together. The cruise line gets away with paying me only $5,000 because that's the post-accident value of the jet ski? That's deplorable."

"Lawmakers never *intended* for limitation law to work this way! The law was *never intended* to protect multibillion dollar cruise lines in the twenty-first century. The law was *intended* to encourage nineteenth century ship owners to engage in trade. The law is being unfairly applied here. And by the way, this cruise line doesn't even register its ships in the United States. I wonder if U.S. lawmakers in 1851 *intended* for this law to protect modern day cruise ships registered in Panama and the Bahamas!" This would certainly leave a judge with a lot to think about.

Successful adaptation can be exercised in many legal situations. This is happening in traffic court, particularly with speeding tickets. In general, speeding tickets are difficult to contest. When a radar gun documents your speed, there's not much evidence a judge cares to see.

Being Adaptive in Obtaining Information In most lawsuits, the plaintiff and defendant turn to each other for information. But in complex legal actions involving public entities, valuable information can be obtained from government records. Under the Freedom of Information Act, plaintiffs can request information from the government, with the exception of the following:

- information authorized by executive order to remain secret (national security)

- information related solely to the internal personnel rules and practices of an agency

- information exempt from disclosure by statute

- certain trade secrets and privileged information

- certain inter-agency and intra-agency memos

- information that would violate personal privacy

- certain law enforcement records

- information related to regulation of financial institutions

- geological and geophysical information

These exceptions are simplified here - the full text appears in 5 U.S.C. Section 552.

She has already heard every excuse under the sun, from chest pains to accelerator malfunction. Take your checkbook and pen out, because the only sound the judge wants to hear from you is the sound of your pen signing a check payable to the department of motor vehicles.

However, some very unique and adaptive arguments have been made regarding speed limit violations. One argument is that speed limits are sometimes set too low for a given stretch of roadway. Some townships arbitrarily choose speed limits, rather than basing them upon sound traffic engineering principles. In response, some motorists have argued that their speeds were NOT too fast for a given stretch of road... but that the speed limit was set too low. This is a unique approach and demonstrates strong powers of adaptation in solving legal problems. Technically, traffic law violators are not plaintiffs. They are defendants. However, the situation is an excellent illustration of legal adaptation in a difficult situation.

Adaptation in nature is essential for survival. Animals that are unable to adapt, whether towards predators or dwindling food sources, become endangered. Likewise, successful plaintiffs must adapt to adversities in the legal system. Let's examine the divorce, a situation which is traditionally painful and expensive, and show how a plaintiff's adaptability can open doors to less expensive and less painful options.

There's no law that says a divorce must be a hate-filled and belligerent process where the parties destroy each other. Mediation is a form of alternate dispute resolution where a mediator helps the parties resolve their dispute. Divorce mediation requires the guidance of someone who is compassionate, while also knowledgeable about divorce law. Traditionally, a divorce is a cruel and destructive affair. It's the legal equivalent of throwing two people into a boxing ring. However, it's a boxing match where both fighters really lose.

Alternate Dispute Resolution, or ADR, is the practice of using alternatives to traditional courtroom litigation in resolving legal disputes. One method of ADR is called *arbitration,* where the parties argue their cases before an arbitrator. An arbitrator is someone with both legal and substantive knowledge of the subject matter. Arbitrators can be former judges, practicing attorneys, or in some cases, non-attorneys who are very knowledgeable about a given subject.

The decision of an arbitrator is binding, which means it has the same effect as the decision of a judge or the verdict of a jury. Arbitration is suitable for many types of disputes, including fee disputes, medical claims, real estate matters, and lost wage claims. An advantage of arbitration is that it's less costly than a trial. It generally takes less time to get an arbitration date than a trial date. The arbitration process is generally less formal than court proceedings, enabling arbitrators to relax the rules of discovery and evidence.

Another ADR technique is *mediation,* which is similar to arbitration, in that the parties argue their dispute before someone with expertise in the subject. But when the decision is made, it is not binding, as is the case with arbitration. Mediation is commonly used in matrimonial matters and labor disputes.

Earlier in the book, I mentioned some of the wrong reasons for becoming a plaintiff. Well, the traditional divorce lawsuit can embody those wrong reasons… hatred, anger, jealousy, or revenge.

But an adaptive plaintiff doesn't fall victim to this human tragedy. An adaptive plaintiff handles this volatile situation by proposing terms for a divorce to the other spouse in a rational manner.

New York Law Makes for Tough Divorces Throughout the United States, a husband and wife can divorce on the grounds of irreconcilable differences. If a marriage is dead and the spouses are unable to sort out their differences, the law mercifully lets them move on. But New York State is special. In New York, a spouse must demonstrate the other is guilty of doing one of the bad things listed below:

- cruel and inhuman treatment that endangers the physical or mental well-being of the victim

- abandonment for a period of one or more years

- imprisonment for three or more consecutive years (following the marriage)

- adultery, which is an act of sexual intercourse voluntarily performed by the defendant with someone other than a spouse

- living apart pursuant to a separation agreement for a period of one or more years

It can be difficult to prove some of the things on this list. That can translate into an expensive divorce. And if a marriage is falling apart for financial reasons, the last thing a couple needs is $40,000 of legal fees heaped on top of their troubles. These types of laws make it all the more important for plaintiffs to be adaptive.

Sometimes it isn't possible to do this if things have deteriorated very badly. But there have been many bitter divorces that took place simply because the spouses didn't think of adapting to the situation by using a less destructive approach. A mediator's role is very different than a divorce attorney's role. A good mediator doesn't take sides or create conflicts of law.

A mediator advises the spouses about what the law requires in terms of maintenance payments, child support, and visitation rights. The mediator tells the spouses they can fight it out, or they can try to hash out terms that are humane for both of them. The bottom line is that if the effort is successful, it's an intelligent legal adaptation that benefits both spouses.

Adaptation is a matter of making do with what you have. The adaptive plaintiff makes lemonade when life gives her lemons. The adaptive plaintiff looks at the law from different angles. The adaptive plaintiff doesn't take anything for granted and doesn't see legal obstacles as being cast in stone. Our justice system itself is not cast in stone. Despite the imposing image of courthouse columns, our justice system operates more on shifting sands than stone foundations.

Laws emerge to fulfill the social and economic needs of the time, depending on who is in control. Laws are not static in nature. They change because of social injustice, public outcry, or safety concerns. On March 25, 1911, a fire took the lives of 146 garment workers in the Triangle Shirtwaist Factory in New York City. The victims were mostly immigrant women who either succumbed to the fire or jumped to their deaths. They died because managers had locked the exits in this dreadful sweatshop.

Like other tragic watershed events, the fire led to laws that called for better safety standards.

We live in an age where new laws are written every day. Some of them are sensible, like those created in the aftermath of the horrible Triangle Shirtwaist Factory fire. And some are questionable in their wisdom. Not all laws are created out of a desire for justice or the public good. Some laws materialize from the zeal of politicians who want to show the public that they're doing something about a problem. Some laws materialize from the ability of special groups to enrich themselves at the expense of the public.

The adaptive plaintiff has the insight to recognize the perversity of badly created laws and argue against them. When a bad law stands in the way of an adaptive plaintiff, she makes arguments that the law is unconstitutional, socially unjust, or against public policy. She also argues about the *legislative intent* of the law. The adaptive plaintiff must be a nimble acrobat, capable of debating a legal issue from many different angles.

What is the lesson of this chapter? A successful plaintiff is adaptable, using creative thinking to overcome obstacles in a lawsuit.

The Successful Plaintiff Conducts Business with Politeness and Professionalism

"So let us begin anew - remembering on both sides that civility is not a sign of weakness, and sincerity is always subject to proof."

John F. Kennedy

It's difficult to criticize an adversary who is polite. People tend to think that legal disputes are resolved by talking tough. That happens in the movies. Successful plaintiffs don't attempt to browbeat the other side into submission.

Theodore Roosevelt said, "Speak softly and carry a big stick." A plaintiff could find herself in a situation where she doesn't hold a big stick. But no plaintiff ever caused herself harm by being courteous and showing respect to the other side.

President John F. Kennedy's quote is all the more profound because of the firm way he handled Soviet Premier Nikita Khrushchev during the Cuban Missile Crisis in 1962. The Soviet Premier saw the former PT Boat commander as a young leader who might be tested. However, President Kennedy assertively stood his ground, walking away from the negotiating table with what he wanted. The result was that Premier Khrushchev pulled his missiles out of Cuba.

Plaintiffs don't accomplish things by pounding their fists on a table. It's one thing to have passion about a case. It's another to act like a jerk. The successful plaintiff doesn't raise her voice when speaking with an adversary. She doesn't make sarcastic comments. She doesn't speak in a condescending tone. The successful plaintiff doesn't try to psych the other side out with foolish games aimed at showing who's in control. The successful plaintiff follows the golden rule and treats the other side as she herself would like to be treated.

Society engrains us to believe that big things are only accomplished by people who act big. This philosophy has deeply permeated its way into the legal profession. We see this in the form of attorneys who feel compelled to act powerful in front of their clients, saying things like, "Let's see how the insurance company acts after a firm like ours slaps them around a little." That attorney knows he has no genuine ability to "slap" around an insurance company. Insurance companies are powerful entities. Their annual revenues exceed the gross national products of many countries. They shape laws and domestic policies. They summarily vanquish opponents with ease. They do NOT get slapped around by plaintiff's attorneys. But yet, a client who hears something like that may think, "Here's someone who will pick up a sword and fight for me!"

Instead of "slapping" any insurance company around, that tough-talking attorney will follow the lessons of this chapter. Some attorneys act flamboyantly because exhibiting confidence is good for bringing in business. It's important for a client to believe his attorney could wrestle alligators and hold lions by the tail. It's important for a client to think of his attorney as a pit bull. But beneath that façade is an attorney who wants to obtain the most favorable resolution of a legal matter with a reasonable investment of effort and resources.

Attorneys aren't evil for thinking this way. Every professional does this. An engineer doesn't design an inland river bridge to withstand ocean typhoons. She designs the bridge to withstand winds in the region, with a reasonable margin of safety. To do otherwise results in a bridge that is needlessly overbuilt and unnecessarily costly. It's a balance of getting the job done and doing it in a cost-effective manner.

When that tough-talking attorney closes the door to his office and gets on the phone with an insurance adjuster, he is humble and polite. He is even charming at times. He's the consummate gentleman when taking care of business. But that's something the client doesn't see, which is better for perpetuating the myth of the pit bull. The lesson here is that more can be accomplished by being polite than roaring like a lion.

The successful plaintiff shows an adversary respect in all forms of interaction, including telephone conversations, letters, e-mails, and meetings. A successful plaintiff speaks to an adversary in a confident and respectful tone of voice. It shouldn't be necessary to say this, but speaker phones are off limits. They have to be among the absolute worst breaches of communications etiquette in any setting, legal or otherwise.

Atticus Finch, a Model Advocate Atticus Finch is one of the main characters in *To Kill a Mockingbird*, the Pulitzer Prize-winning novel by Harper Lee. Atticus Finch was brought to life by Gregory Peck in the 1962 film version of the novel.

Atticus Finch is honest, decent, and brave. He is soft-spoken, yet possessed of a legal mind that cuts like a surgeon's knife. *To Kill A Mockingbird* is set in Alabama during the Great Depression. In the story, a black man is accused of raping a white woman. Atticus Finch is appointed by the court to defend the accused man, which pits local residents against him and his family. Despite Atticus's best efforts, the jury convicts his client.

The character of Atticus Finch has inspired many young women and men to enter the legal profession. In legal circles, he symbolizes the ideal advocate.

By using a speaker phone, a person says, "I'm more important than you. As we speak, I'll tap away at my keyboard. You don't deserve my full attention." No one at the other end of a speaker phone ever thought, "I'm very impressed by the way this person is handling me... he must be important." The sentiments are usually more along the lines of, "What an obnoxious a____e!" And I'll leave it to readers to guess the word I've left out. It isn't *advocate!*

Just as with telephone manners, a code of conduct governs a successful plaintiff's tone in writing letters and other correspondence. A legal letter should be well-written. It should be free of grammatical and spelling errors. It should be respectful, yet make its point. In terms of sentence structure, try to use declaratory sentences. Avoid sentences that take the form of questions. For instance, do not write, *"When do you plan to make payment on iron pipe I delivered to your plumbing shop?"* Instead, write, *"Please advise when you plan to make payment on iron pipe I delivered to your plumbing shop."*

Before writing he first sentence of a letter, a successful plaintiff outlines the relevant facts. This is the most time-consuming aspect of preparing a legal letter because it requires reconstruction of a timeline of events. There are a number of different formats legal letters may take, each needing to be tailored to the situation at hand. However, a common denominator of all good legal letters is that they outline the basic facts in a dispute and state what the defendant is liable for, e.g., breaching a contract, or damaging a fence. A legal letter should provide a demand. The demand can be in the form of a dollar figure or a request for performance, such as the repair of a sidewalk.

A legal letter should be direct and unambiguous. If a plaintiff needs a reply before a specific date, he should state that. In the interest of expediting a dialogue, the letter can request that the adversary contact the plaintiff. Whether or not it does this, the letter should contain correct contact information. It's helpful to include a correct e-mail address and telephone number in addition to a traditional street address.

In general, a legal letter should have an assertive and firm tone. It can be polite at the same time. This can be accomplished by including a sentence to the effect of, *"I'm hopeful we can resolve this matter to preserve our longstanding business relationship."* That can get the message across that a plaintiff wishes to be amicable, but that she also means business. Being polite isn't a sign of weakness. Some letters take a threatening tone, as in, *"Please be advised that if we do not hear from you within twenty days, we will commence legal action."* There's obviously no ambiguity there. The intentions are clearly expressed. However, there can be a peril in writing something along those lines, because a threat that isn't fulfilled can ultimately weaken the position of the person making the threat.

In addition to conversations and correspondence, a successful plaintiff acts with politeness and professionalism in face-to-face meetings. When meeting with an adversary, the successful plaintiff dresses to create a favorable impression and show respect. We live in a world where the traditional suit and tie have almost become symbols of stiffness and ridicule. Although many workplaces have loosened dress codes to Casual Friday mode, a plaintiff doesn't show weakness by dressing professionally to meet with an adversary. A judge never thought less of a plaintiff for wearing a shirt and tie instead of a polo shirt.

For women, a conservative dress or suit is a good choice. This isn't a book about fashion tips for the legal world. But a meeting with a legal adversary shares similarities with a job interview. The goal is not to get a job offer, but to make a favorable impression in presenting a legal position. Like a job interview, most men wouldn't go without socks or skip shaving for two days. Most women wouldn't dress as if they were going to a dance club on a Saturday night. There's a time and place for every type of attire, and a meeting with a legal adversary is a time to dress appropriately.

The successful plaintiff is professional and courteous in demeanor. That doesn't mean she's a sap. She understands that spoken words and e-mails can't be taken back. In criminal law, there's something called a *Miranda warning*. Named for the landmark case of *Miranda v. Arizona*, the warning is supposed to be recited to criminal suspects. A police officer is supposed to tell a suspect:

- You have the right to remain silent.

- Anything you say or do can, and will, be used against you.

- You have the right to speak with an attorney.

- If you cannot afford an attorney, one will be appointed for you.

The reason for the warning is that a person who has been apprehended by police could be in an excited and unsettled state of mind. The person might blurt out the first thing that comes to mind, which could be incriminating. It's important for police to properly administer the warning. Otherwise, the suspect's defense attorney could argue that their client's Miranda rights were violated.

Obviously, there aren't any such warnings when it comes to non-criminal legal matters. Maybe there should be, because there are times when it's best to say what is necessary, without saying more. A successful plaintiff knows that. A successful plaintiff realizes that when an adversary or the adversary's attorney asks questions, it isn't to help the plaintiff's position.

If a defendant can get a plaintiff to appear uncertain in a line of questioning, the defendant knows that's a good thing. If a defendant can get a plaintiff to contradict herself, that's even better. And if a defendant can get a plaintiff to lie on the witness stand, that's a real prize for the defendant. In legal terms, that's called *perjury*, which is the act of lying under oath. Perjury itself is a crime, independent of the underlying legal proceedings. Perjury carries criminal penalties. Needless to say, it also demolishes the plaintiff's credibility.

Acting with professionalism in telephone conversations, correspondence, and face-to-face meetings is important. It's also critical to be organized, which is part of being professional. Although it's considered a courtesy to offer copies of well-organized records for a defendant to review, defendants like it more when a plaintiff is disorganized.

That's why it's crucial for plaintiffs to keep records of everything relevant to their legal matter. Legal actions often come down to a matter of records. Both sides in a lawsuit may have good merits in their positions. But other things being equal, the side with the best records wins. When you think about all the things that can stand in the way of being a successful plaintiff, sloppy recordkeeping is an easy pitfall to avoid.

The Side with the Best Records Often Prevails The importance of recordkeeping is not lost upon corporate human resources departments, where keeping tabs on employees is a creed. Employees should realize that everything they do at work is electronically documented. This includes the times they enter and leave the workplace, log on to and log out of computers, send e-mails, search the internet, and use telephones.

It's difficult to beat the recordkeeping abilities of a large organization.

The element of professionalism is broader than a plaintiff's conduct DURING a legal action. It also includes her conduct BEFORE a legal action. At the beginning of this book, I mentioned that it's important to pick one's legal battles. That means legal situations must be evaluated on their *merits*. But you'd be surprised how many plaintiffs overlook this rule. That's because they might be looking to wage a legal battle for the *wrong reasons*.

As human beings, we're not perfect. We're subject to our emotions. These include anger, hatred, envy, revenge, or jealousy. Those are disastrous reasons for starting a legal battle. A legal battle initiated for the *wrong reasons* fails the test of professionalism, as well as the test of picking battles wisely. A legal action launched for the wrong reasons is an invitation to unnecessary headaches and expense.

What is the lesson of this chapter? A successful plaintiff who acts with politeness and professionalism earns dividends in terms of successful negotiations and effective dispute resolution.

The Successful Plaintiff Enjoys Some Element of Luck

"Fortune brings in some boats that are not steered."

William Shakespeare

By now, you probably have good insight into what it takes to be a successful plaintiff. We've covered a lot of ground together. However, there's something that can affect a plaintiff's success as profoundly as all the personal qualities discussed throughout this book. Seeing the quote above, you know I'm talking about the element of *luck*. Luck can play a large role in the making of a successful plaintiff.

If you saw the movie *A Few Good Men*, you wouldn't be likely to forget the riveting scene at the end where Colonel Nathan Jessep, played by Jack Nicholson, is being questioned by Lieutenant Daniel Kaffee, played by Tom Cruise. He becomes increasingly antagonized as Tom Cruise asks him questions about the death of a young private on a Marine Corps base. When Tom Cruise steps up the intensity of his questioning, Jack Nicholson reaches the breaking point and yells, "You can't handle the truth!" It was an unexpected prize for the prosecution that the colonel should come undone on the witness stand. Talk about luck. Although Hollywood isn't real life, that memorable scene shows that luck can deliver things that aren't expected in some legal settings.

Luck can play a larger role in a lawsuit than many attorneys would like to admit. Imagine the glowing jubilation of an attorney who wins a million dollar award in a personal injury case. Over drinks at the bar, he tells his buddies about his exploits in the courtroom. His buddies listen to how he skewered defense witnesses during cross-examination. His buddies listen to how he researched obscure appellate court decisions in putting together the most brilliant legal brief ever written, and how the judge asked him if he ever considered a career as a law professor. He doesn't tell his buddies that the police officer responding to the accident wrote a report that made the case a slam dunk. He doesn't tell his buddies that the radiologist interpreting the MRIs sealed the outcome of the case with a diagnosis of a herniated disc in the cervical spine.

It's human nature to downplay the role that luck plays in our accomplishments. It's more satisfying to let everyone think we're brilliant on those occasions that the stars shine upon us. Luck can arise in so many different aspects of a lawsuit that it's difficult to count them. However, when it comes to legal strategy and tactics, it's possible to identify a few areas where luck can play a significant role.

Jurisdiction This is the element of where a legal action will take place. It can make a difference because laws differ from one state to another. This includes both substantive and procedural laws. For instance, in New York, the statute of limitations for bringing a lawsuit for injuries in a car accident lawsuit is three years. In New Jersey, it's two years. If a plaintiff fails act to within two years, New York law gives them a break. New Jersey law doesn't.

Substantive Law versus Procedural Law Legal scholars classify laws under two major headings, *substantive* law and *procedural* law. Substantive law defines the rights and duties of the parties in a legal matter. *Cause of action* is an example of substantive law. Is the case a negligence cause of action? Is it a breach of contract cause of action? Those things are determined by substantive law.

Procedural law addresses guidelines to be followed in a legal action. The rules of evidence determine which pieces of information are admissible in court, and are considered procedural law. The rules of civil procedure govern certain timetables to be followed by the parties in a lawsuit. For instance, a defendant might have to reply to a plaintiff's summons and complaint within 20 days if served personally, or within 30 days if served by mail. This is an example of procedural law.

Venue The successful plaintiff may pick her battles, but she doesn't always get to pick her battlefield. The element of venue determines the county where a legal matter will be heard. Venue is determined by the rules of civil procedure. The county where a case is heard can make a difference in the outcome of a lawsuit, due to social, political, and economic backgrounds of jurors.

The Judge People regard the judge as a referee of justice, guiding legal proceedings with fairness and equality. However, judges are human beings and have their likes and dislikes. They have their peeves and prejudices. Obtaining a law degree doesn't make one a saint. Attorneys generally become judges through election or appointment. In a jury trial, a judge doesn't decide a case. She gives instructions to jurors about the facts and issues they must weigh in arriving at a verdict. She decides disputes that arise between attorneys. She maintains order. However, she is a human being and not a computer. As such, the personal qualities of a judge can impart tremendous influence on the outcome of a lawsuit.

Defense Attorney Which law firm will be selected by the defendant to defend against your case? Whichever firm it turns out to be, it isn't something you have control over. If the firm is small and aggressive, you could be in for a nasty fight. The attorneys in the firm might want to achieve a reputation for being extraordinarily tough, where you become an unfortunate stepping stone in their professional ambitions. They could act like total psychopaths, stopping at nothing to have your case thrown out of court, all in the interest of developing a reputation for being legal pit bulls. On the other hand, a defense attorney could be friendly. She might feel that there's no need to conduct legal proceedings with hostility and animosity. Whatever the case may be, this is an element of a lawsuit that hinges on luck.

Jurors A jury is sometimes described as twelve pairs of shoes. I don't think the description is meant to be insulting towards jurors. I think it only serves to show that a jury is a panel of people over whom you have no control.

Twelve Angry Men This 1957 black and white film is considered a classic legal drama. The story takes place in the stark confines of a jury deliberation room.

The story centers on twelve jurors who struggle to reach a unanimous verdict in a criminal case. A teenage boy from an inner city slum is on trial for the murder of his father. The jurors are instructed by the judge that if they find the boy *guilty*, the death sentence is mandatory. In a preliminary vote, eleven of the twelve jurors vote *guilty*, with Henry Fonda playing the lone juror who votes *not guilty*. He expresses his concerns that evidence against the boy is largely circumstantial, and that he has doubts about the credibility of the two witnesses. In the deliberations that follow, other jurors eventually change their votes to *not guilty*.

The movie depicts human prejudices and weaknesses, and shows how jurors are easily governed by their personal dislikes. When one juror changes his vote to not guilty just so he won't miss a baseball game that night, it is a low point for the jury. The movie is a stark portrait of the institution of jury duty. It shows that the lives of criminal defendants can often be in the hands of jurors who simply hate them for what they are, jurors who are troubled by their own personal issues, or jurors who just don't care. However, the movie also conveys the message that some jurors take their civic responsibility of jury duty seriously.

There is control in the process of selecting jurors. In the *voir dire* process, meaning to "speak the truth," plaintiffs and defendants get the opportunity to question prospective jurors to determine if they would like to have them eliminated from a case. This can happen if the plaintiff or defendant senses something in a juror that could make them biased.

Although jury duty is an important civic responsibility, it has come to be regarded as a nuisance by many. Some people see jury duty as a headache that can jeopardize job security with a good employer. Therefore, many prospective jurors answer questions with the intention of getting disqualified from duty. You thought attorneys were smart. They're no match for clever jurors who want to get off jury duty! At any rate, the point is that the quality and integrity of jurors who decide your case can be a matter of luck.

All these factors demonstrate that there will always be things that can't be controlled by plaintiffs in their legal affairs. This list is far from exhaustive. We're all familiar with Murphy's Law, which says that if something can go wrong, it will. A successful plaintiff plans for the operation of Murphy's Law and other contingencies. She leaves as little to chance as possible. She makes her own luck by preparing thoroughly. And as for the other factors, she tells herself that there's no point stressing over things you can't control.

What is the lesson of this chapter? Despite a plaintiff's best efforts to control things in a lawsuit or other legal matter, some things simply come down to luck.

Conclusion

"I like the dreams of the future better than the history of the past."

Thomas Jefferson

We've covered a lot of ground together in this short book. I hope the experience was as enjoyable as it was informative. I hope you walk away with meaningful insight about how to navigate our legal system as a successful plaintiff.

However, I'd like readers to keep something in mind. Legal matters tend to be complex in nature. They can involve many variables and unexpected twists. As a plaintiff, you try to do the best with what you have. You prepare diligently. You plan for the worse, but hope for the best. You take a deep breath and put your best foot forward.

Throughout all these discussions about the qualities of successful plaintiffs, I left out one quality. That's because I wanted to save it for the end. That quality is this. Most plaintiffs *would rather not have been plaintiffs*. If they could, most would turn back time to undo the events that caused them to become plaintiffs.

But it isn't possible to undo the past. Life, like history, marches forward in one direction. And if there's a lesson to be learned here, it's that successful plaintiffs don't deplete their energy worrying about what happened in the past. They look ahead with hope and optimism to achieve victory in a legal struggle. In other words, what's done is done… move on and make the best of the battle.

I know the role of plaintiff is a tough spot to be in. But if you ever find yourself in that spot, I hope the things you learn in this book will help you in that role. I hope this book may give you inspiration to hold your own against life's adversities and injustices.

Good luck!

Twelve Qualities of the Successful Plaintiff

Tamara Kismet

Disclaimer

No book that deals with the subject of law makes it past the editors of a publishing house without a disclaimer. So here it is:

The information in this book is provided as general information only. It is not offered as legal advice and is not intended to be legal advice. No one should act, or refrain from acting, based upon the information in this book.

Laws, regulations, statutes, court decisions, or other information in this book are not provided as legal reference materials, and are not intended to serve as legal reference materials. Readers are cautioned to verify the content, completeness, accuracy, and current disposition of any laws, regulations, statutes, court decisions, or other legal information that appears in this book.

The author makes no representations or warranties about information contained in this book. Readers are advised to consult with a competent attorney for questions they may have about the law.

Tamara Kismet

ABOUT THE AUTHOR

The author teaches business law in an adjunct capacity, and is an attorney with close to twenty years of experience in the litigation and arbitration of complex cases.

www.ingramcontent.com/pod-product-compliance
Lightning Source LLC
Chambersburg PA
CBHW051530170526
45165CB00002B/680